Our
research
with pyra-
mid models led
us to the writing of
*The Secret Power of
Pyramids.* But the ad-
venture did not end there.
Something happened. People
were amazed, looked again, and
this glance inspired a new journey
not easy to abandon. Our research
goes on; it has only begun. No sooner had
we finished the first book than we found ourselves on the threshold of new discoveries. This
book is about those discoveries.—THE AUTHORS

THE PSYCHIC POWER OF PYRAMIDS

by Bill Schul & Ed Pettit

A FAWCETT GOLD MEDAL BOOK

Fawcett Publications, Inc., Greenwich, Connecticut

THE PSYCHIC POWER OF PYRAMIDS

Permission granted for reproduction and publication data on SEO
experiment #76-001 OPERATION RAZOR BLADE by Charles
W. Dutreau.

Plans for house by permission of Heritage Homes Plan Service,
Inc., 3030 Peachtree Road NE, Atlanta, Georgia 30305

ISBN 0-449-13845-3

Printed in the United States of America

10   9   8   7   6   5   4   3   2   1

Contents

Foreword

What kind of person would write a book like this? What kind of person would read a book like this?

Perhaps these questions can be answered by words which are engraved on a plaque that hangs on the wall of my office just above my desk. The words, attributed to the Greek slave-philosopher Epictetus, are:

It is impossible for anyone to begin to learn what he thinks he already knows.

Yes, you, the reader of this book, and Bill Schul and Ed Pettit, the authors, share an all too rare quality—the willingness to admit there are things you do not know. And, you must also have the capacity to wonder about your world, your universe, and yourself.

Whether or not anything in this book ever proves to have a sound scientific basis is, to me, relatively unimportant. What is important is that Bill Schul and Ed Pettit have provided a vehicle for further stimulating the wonderment of each person who reads what has been written here. And the more you wonder, the less you are afraid to say "I don't know," the more you will allow yourself to discover.

HUGH R. RIORDAN, M.D.

Introduction

DEAR BILL and ED:

"You likely have sustained some flak from some who have read your book. I was about to write you one of those letters but decided, in all fairness, to try a pyramid beforehand. I'm glad that I did because—whatever the causes, whatever the reasons—something does happen inside of pyramids. Will write you later about some of the results, but just wanted to say that the best reply you can give to your critics is, 'Try it.'

"Gratefully,
T.J.
Rochester, Minnesota"

"In your book *The Secret Power of Pyramids* you mention the use of water charged in a pyramid as a facial lotion. Well, I have suspected for some time that many of the cosmetics on the market are harmful to the skin, at least with prolonged use. For the past four weeks I have used nothing but pyramid water on my face . . . Maybe it's positive thinking, maybe it's just giving my skin a chance to breathe again, but whatever, my skin hasn't looked this good in twenty years!

> "Sincerely,
> Mrs. C.M.
> Miami, Florida"

In *The Secret Power of Pyramids* we invited readers to write us if they had any questions or information they would like to share. We were not to be ignored.

Some of the letters were of the enjoyed-your-book-and-wish-you-well sort, certainly to be appreciated, but many of the notes described experiments. "What's happening?" some asked. "I constructed a pyramid according to your plans, put some water under it for a time, and now the water is doing all kinds of fantastic things . . ."

Some of the phenomena described are familiar to us but certainly not all. The ingenuity of the human mind is the most astounding phenomena of all. Sometimes the most creative projects are those designed by persons with little formal education in the physical sciences, such as the twelve-year-old youngster who told us that he was testing the life span of houseflies in pyramids and other containers. A fifty-year-old steelworker, who claimed only five years of schooling, wrote to us that he was closely watching the behavior patterns of ants in a hill over which he had placed a pyramid as compared to another anthill a short distance away. He is also planning to place pyramids over half of his ten beehives. These creative individuals may well come up with some valuable reports.

One is reminded of the story of Bill Lear, inventor of the car radio, the eight-track stereo, the Learjet, and many other things. Lear, who has little formal education, stated that he was able to accomplish these feats because he didn't know they couldn't be done.

We don't always know what the letter writers have done in their experiments. Maybe they have inadvertently or by design altered some component of an experiment in such a fashion as to produce a different result. It may be of no consequence; it may be of great significance. There is a need to explore further and we write asking them to supply further details.

For the most part, the writers describe results confirmed or confirmable by others. Such reports are helpful, as they reflect a consistency in phenomena occurrence. But the bizarre . . . arms levitating inside pyramids, objects materializing, the occurrence of strange light . . . the product of hallucination? mental aberrations? imagination? How can we evaluate these experiences; they did not occur to us. We might say that if these events happened, they did so for other reasons than pyramid influence. Yet, how do we know? Maybe their pyramids are different from our pyramids; certainly the writers are different people. Perhaps the phenomena they report are just as explainable as sharpening razor blades, at least to some people.

We tend to like tidy little reports that fit neatly within the perimeters of our understanding of forces at work in the universe. We talk about the movement of molecules and the interaction of energy fields and think that in doing so we have offered a rational explanation of why things behave the way they do. If somebody were to say that his pyramid destroyed an apple instead of preserving it, we would prefer to shuffle the heretical report to the bottom of the pile and not think about it. We are used to thinking of pyramids preserving things. Instead, we should be listening to our inner voices saying, "In order to understand pyramid energy you may have to readjust your ideas of physical laws."

There may be something sacred about the design and purpose of the pyramids, but there is nothing sacred about our views concerning them. We have to be open in our appraisal of every report we receive and every opinion offered, and this includes that of the individual who states that the pyramid is a spaceship and wonders why we haven't understood this all along. It was Einstein who said that anything that *can* happen in the universe *will* happen in the universe. What we refer to as physical law is not truth *qua* truth; it is merely our ideas of how things work. Inasmuch as our observations are limited, the manner in which we perceive cannot possibly be the correct one. Physical law is subject to the intellectual growth of the observer and isn't going to be the same tomorrow as it is today. The moral of the story is openness to new ways of looking at things. What we say about pyramid behavior isn't what we'll be saying next year or five years from now, or we've missed the message in the experiments. All we have to say at this time is that this is the evidence. Further, we can offer some interpretation drawn from our own knowledge and experience, and after that we can say, "Okay, now you know what we know and the rest is up to you."

Some people insist on closure. They feel psychologically insecure unless the gate is closed. Questions without answers frighten them and they will assign answers regardless of how indefensible they may be. Their vested interest is security and greater truth is not worth the gamble. It is difficult for such people to consider that truth, to the extent that we can understand it, is dynamic and not static. As Einstein put it, "As far as the laws of mathematics refer to reality, they are not certain; and so far as they are certain, they do not refer to reality."

When somebody writes to us and says, "Sitting inside the pyramid, I understand the secrets of the universe," who are we to pass judgment on his experience? If he asks, we can suggest that he submit his "truths" to further examination and application and endeavor to remain open to alternative explanations. We might even harbor some suspicion that our correspondent is laboring under delusions, but it is not our task to assign conclusions. Better, perhaps, for us to remember that direct or intuitive knowing is a reality. Einstein attested to this when he stated that he did not reason out the theory of relativity but that it came to him.

A Toledo, Ohio, housewife wrote us and explained that her husband had constructed a wood-frame, plastic-covered pyramid in a spare bedroom and they were using it for meditation. But, she said, "while we find that meditation is usually easier inside the pyramid, there are occasions when I experience a mild form of nausea. Can you offer an explanation for this?"

There are a couple of possible explanations. According to Dr. John Pierrakos, a New York psychiatrist, each cell, tissue, and organ of the body has an optimal vibratory rate. In the case of illness, fatigue, and so on, this pulsation drops below the level necessary for good health. The task, then, of the therapist is to raise the beat or pulsation to a higher level. If the pyramid is a resonator of energy fields, it may be stimulating the cells and tissues to a higher level of functioning. The body may be experiencing some adjustment to this excitation. However, as far as is known, the subtle influence of the pyramid will not stimulate the cells, tissue, and so on beyond their normal optimal level. This is not to say that caution shouldn't be exercised. Until we know more, the wisest choice might be to move outside the pyramid when this sensation is experienced.

Acupuncture has led us to believe that the body has an electrical flow separate from nerve current. Illness or distress is caused when the current becomes blocked in one of the meridians. Acupuncture with the needles or acupressure massage can be used to eliminate this block. Occasionally this treatment will cause mild nausea. Apparently it is not serious and usually quickly passes. It is possible that the energy field inside the pyramid can behave in a manner similar to acupuncture.

Other considerations should include biorhythm, biochemical factors, perhaps allergic reactions to material used in the pyramid's construction, and negative thoughts or feelings in conflict with the pyramid's positive fields. Several metaphysical systems teach certain exercises to be used when the body is too negative, and other exercises when the body is overly positive.

As plastic is cheap and easy to work with, it has become

a popular covering for larger pyramids. However, in Bill Kerrell's and Kathy Goggin's *The Guide to Pyramid Energy* reference is made to a NASA report that plastic inside space vehicles absorbs and blocks the passage of negative ions.

An ion is an electrified particle formed when a neutral atom or group of atoms loses or gains one or more electrons.

"The Agency's space scientists have determined that negative and positive ions have a vital effect on human physical and mental well-being. In particular, negative ions have a beneficial effect, while an excess of positive ions has a harmful, depressing effect," Kerrell and Goggin state.

While we have found that plants and algae thrive under plastic pyramids, the reactions of humans are not so easily determined inasmuch as there are so many variables to consider and the alteration of the field by plastics may be very subtle. Obviously, there is room here for additional research. There are variations in plastics, and biochemists such as Dr. Roger J. Williams, University of Texas, has made us aware of the wide differences in individual biochemistry. In any case, it would be well for us to focus attention on any information that may provide deeper insights into pyramid phenomena.

Quite a large number of people have written us with questions on construction of pyramids. Some say they have problems deciphering the information in our book or plans obtained elsewhere. We want everyone interested in pyramids not to become discouraged because of problems over angles and so on. Therefore, we are including at the back of this book a small pattern and instructions on how it can be used for making pyramids of any size.

We have received several letters from people asking if meditating in pyramids will contribute to their psychic development. The following letter from a junior high school music instructor in New Mexico is representative:

"When I was a child, my powers of mental telepathy were pretty good, so good, in fact, that it frightened me. I forced myself to ignore the messages and, of course, the talent seemed to fade away. Now I think I have matured enough to handle it but the talent doesn't seem to be there any more. I'm looking for techniques to improve not only my mental telepathy but also other ESP skills. Do you think the pyramid would help?"

We replied, "Most people who experienced psychic powers when children find that it is comparatively easy to renew these skills with some effort and practice. But you should consider very carefully your ability to handle the extra sensitivity, awareness of other people's thoughts, feelings, heartaches, tragedies, along with the positive things that will bombard you. Added awareness brings with it tremendous responsibilities and it makes great demands upon a person's physical, emotional, and mental strengths, and therefore requires tremendous inner poise and stability. This is the reason that all of the world's great teachers speak of mental and spiritual growth rather than psychic development, knowing that with the development toward the higher self psychic skills will also emerge but will be seen as secondary. The individual is thus more prepared to handle added senses. As to whether the pyramid will contribute to your psychic development, this is for the most part an individual matter and dependent upon inclinations, desire, effort, etc., but there are reasons to believe that pyramid space is conducive to inner scanning."

Many of the letters we receive are from people who simply have experienced some interesting things as a result of pyramid research and they wish to pass this information along. Following are quotes from some of the letters:

"I own my own truck and occasionally make long-distance hauls. Have found in recent years that I have a difficult time staying awake after dark and this works a real hardship in not being able to make the time that I should. I can't handle too much coffee and I certainly don't want to take anything else. Well, I read your book, built my own pyramid and started sleeping in it part of the time and particularly before I make a long haul. Now I can get along on fewer hours of sleep—more rested, I guess—and

I'm not a menace on the highway. Fact of the matter is, I now put pyramid water in one of my Thermos bottles."

"I no sooner had my pyramid built than my teenage son copped on to it and hauled it off to his room where he and his friends try different things. Told him to build his own pyramid; got the same result as when I ask him to mow the lawn. Well, I had to get another telephone, so now I guess I'll have to build another pyramid."

"Every winter I come down with colds even though I take vitamin supplements. This winter, however, I started meditating twice a day in a six-foot plastic pyramid and my fringe benefit is that I haven't even experienced a sniffle."

"I am a heavy-equipment operator and I used to come home so beat at the end of the day all I wanted to do was plop in a chair and stare at the television set. My kids would want me to play catch, games, or take them somewhere and nine out of ten times I wouldn't budge from my overstuffed chair. Now when I come home the first thing I do is sit in my outside wooden pyramid for about thirty minutes. I feel like I've rested several hours and I'm ready to do something with the family."

"I started back to college after being away from it for many years. I wondered at first if I would be able to hack it and for the first few months I had a difficult time keeping pace. Part of it I'm sure was the need to adjust but I feel certain that sitting in a pyramid to read and study made all the difference in the world. Now I can read for many hours on end with no trouble being distracted."

"I retired recently from a very active business career. My wife and I had saved our money and we made some wise investments so money was not a problem. Our problem was that we soon became bored. We had never developed any real hobbies that we could pursue—my wife had also worked—so we were at a loss as to what direction to turn. Then we happened to come upon your book *The Secret Power of Pyramids,* which was recommended to us by a friend. We became so fascinated in the experiments that we built a pyramid, then another pyramid, and now

Sherry Fennell, Ed Pettit's daughter, in door of pyramid.

we have pyramids all over the place. Not only that, but we have become so interested in the whole field that we are now planning trips to Mexico and Central America to visit the pyramids there, along with some of the old ruins, and we may even go to Egypt . . ."

"I have been involved in biofeedback training for three years. I went into training because I was having a difficult time getting anywhere with meditation. I started with the skin-temperature machine and after gaining some success and confidence with it I switched over to a portable alpha-theta brainwave sensor. I now teach brainwave training part time at our local college and have given a few talks on the subject to interested groups. When I learned of the work being done with pyramids, I became involved in learning what I could and soon built several pyramids. One of the pyramids was large enough to meditate in. In the meantime, I had developed sufficiently in my own brain-wave training that I was able to produce quite a few low-frequency alpha states and some theta. But, strangely enough, my production of alpha-theta waves jumped considerably after I started using the pyramid. I am now running tests on several volunteers, using the biofeedback devices outside and inside the pyramid. I run a volunteer outside the pyramid one day and inside the next. With very few exceptions the subject is able to produce more alpha-theta inside the pyramid, and we have tested most of the subjects a number of times."

"When my plant experiments proved to my satisfaction that something unusual was happening inside pyramids, I decided to try some time-lapse photography as described in your book. At this time I'm just in the process of setting it up but I will let you know of the results. I feel sure that the plants will show a different behavior inside than outside the pyramid but I'll try to keep this bias from affecting my experiments."

"I don't think you will remember me but I heard you speak several years ago about yogic breathing and how important it was to learn to breathe correctly. You warned us then not to try complicated breathing without an accomplished teacher and many hours of preparation. I took your counseling seriously and have not regretted it, but I did find someone who could teach me how to breathe and I have become a serious student of Yoga pranayama. The reason I am mentioning this to you in a letter is because I have found that breathing exercises are more effective if done inside pyramids. This may be my imagination, but I don't think so, for several of my students have said the same thing. I still agree with you, however, that while simple deep-breathing exercises are fine and definitely worthwhile, no one should undertake some of the more complicated exercises without a teacher."

As we have asked experimenters to write us about their findings, we believe this information should be shared with others and the contents of other letters or the ideas presented have been incorporated in appropriate chapters throughout the book.

## 1

The Invisible Pyramid

Our research and that of others with pyramid models led us to the writing of *The Secret Power of Pyramids*. But the adventure did not end there. We were to learn that one does not initiate pyramid research to satisfy an idle moment's curiosity. Something happens. One is amazed, looks again, and this glance embarks one upon a journey not easy to abandon. Our research goes on; likely it has only begun. No sooner had we finished the first book than we found ourselves on the threshold of new discoveries. Where and when will it end? We suspect that one starts out looking for the pyramids of the universe and ends up crawling through the passageways of oneself.

"Suppose there is still another answer to the ruins in the rain forests of Yucatán, or to the incised brick tablets baking under the Mesopotamian sun. Suppose that greater than all these, vaster and more impressive, an invisible pyramid lies at the heart of every civilization man has created, that for every visible brick or corbeled vault or upthrust skyscraper or giant rocket we bear a burden in the mind to excess; that we have a biological urge to complete what is actually uncompletable."

The invisible pyramid . . . perhaps the huge Egyptian monolith haunting man's memory of a forgotten wisdom is only a crystallized shadow of a perfect pyramid within. Perhaps—as anthropologist Dr. Loren Eiseley has hinted in the above passage—what we are looking for is the pyramid that existed in the minds of those ancient dreamers as they raised their stone on the Gizeh plain. Was this vision, so perfectly held, translatable in a limestone mountain? To what extent did they consider themselves successful in materializing the forms within their minds? Where are those mental constructs now? Upon what plane could they retain their immortality? Is not the reason we struggle with and dig and measure the stone pyramid that we cannot get at the one within the builder's mind? Which one is it that we are really interested in? Isn't it really the invisible one that we seek?

If by some quirk of genetic memory tracing we could get back to that mind, or by some luck of reincarnative detective work we found that architect's mind living and well in Burbank, California, or Tallahassee, Florida, would we really be so interested in probing for hidden clues among the rocks?

Isn't it that we want to know what the Great Pyramid knows? And better still, we want to know what the designer of the pyramid knew, for can we assume that he was totally successful in imparting in his construction everything that he wished when no poet, composer, scientist, or artist since that time has so completely succeeded?

The Great Pyramid stands as a great, unforgettable monument to a lost knowledge. We are sure—perhaps due more to mystical stirrings than concrete evidence—that incorporated within its ageless walls are secrets of many wondrous things that someday will be yielded up.

For a while we believed the puzzle could be unraveled with hammer and chisel and we were wrong. For a time we were certain the code could be broken with tape measure, algebra, and compass, and we were deluded. Later still we imagined that this largest of man-made Pandora's boxes could be deciphered with sonar and stripline recorders, but alas, to no avail.

Yet, one message came (or perhaps was allowed) through. The shape of the pyramid was a segment of the puzzle. The discovery that small pyramids constructed according to the design of the Great Pyramid and also aligned on the north-south axis would produce unusual phenomena suddenly cast the search in a new light: the pyramid was universal, that is, the knowledge to be gained was not limited to dark passageways in Egypt. The quest became personalized and extended to curious seekers everywhere. But the greatest shift came in the manner in which the exploration could be undertaken: One need not go to Egypt with shovel, slide rule and a guide to hieroglyphics. It was to be brought home to one's own environment, one's own life-space, where it could be perceived in all of its ramifications and with all of its vast implications. Here its knowledge could be applied, not just to the profound lore of Egyptian academia but also to the everyday tasks and problems—health, food, energy—faced by you and me and our next-door neighbor.

Finally, it must lead us to the source for all our answers, the higher self within.

While sitting in a Los Angeles café with Cleve Backster—the polygraph expert who startled the scientific community several years ago with his announcement that plants have an emotional response—he told me that when the plant reacted to threats of its well-being as recorded on his modified polygraph he experienced a sudden elevation in consciousness. The world had never been quite the same since, Backster said.

"Where do you live? On Park Avenue, or on Dixon; on the hill, in the valley, in the city, or in the country? In your body?" asks Harold E. Kohn in the book *Reflections*. "The real you is not the house you live in, or even the body that you inhabit, or in anything that can be measured or weighed or described in terms of color or texture. Your real home is invisible. Your interests and wants, your thoughts and your purposes are where you really live; but you have never seen an interest, a want, a thought or a purpose, but only what these invisible values can do with visible things. We see the birdhouse a boy makes, but the interest in birds and carpentry that prompted him to make it are invisible. A church building is apparent, but the more important things about a church are incapable of being seen. The faith that forms the fellowship of kindred minds, the inner spiritual cravings that bring people to worship remain beyond sensory perception. Houses are seen, but the love that makes a house a home is invisible. We must live in the unseen if we are to live at all . . ."

Pyramid research is building models with correct measurements out of wood or plastic or glass or whatever. It is the observing of the behavior of metal and plants and liquids, perhaps anything you like. But more importantly it is the observation of yourself—your reactions inside a pyramid, yes, but also while studying everything else.

Astronaut Edgar Mitchell left the space program after he walked on the moon as a member of the 1971 Apollo 14 lunar expedition. The reason he gave was that the exploration of outer space was less important to the welfare of mankind than the exploration of inner space. Speaking at a recent meeting of the American Psychiatric Association in Dallas, Texas, he said that he was quite sure we had reached that historical time when we could push the boundaries of scientific knowledge little further without a more thorough knowledge of that which observed it.

Mitchell made it quite clear that the old scientific tradition of the experimenter remaining aloof from his experiment could no longer be preserved. "It has been clearly demonstrated," he said, "that the experimenter is a component of the experiment," and that this insight would have to be incorporated within a new scientific paradigm.

This new arrangement in scientific exploration—the examiner as an ingredient—came about as the result of technological advances of recent years. Mystics and clairvoyants had for centuries talked about the singular nature of all living things—that being of one unified substance everything was interrelated and change in one unit had a large or small reaction on all units. But there was little in this interesting speculation that would lend itself to the hard, objective data required by science.

The ancient Indian spoke of this universal substance as "prana" and the Chinese talk about "Chi"; later Mesmer described "animal magnetism," Von Reichenbach discussed "odic force," and Reich spoke of "orgone energy"; and today we are using such terms as "bioplasmic energy" and "psychotronic energy." But now this X-force has been hauled into the laboratory, thanks to the development of instruments that will allow us to measure subtle energy fields and amplify and monitor the psychophysiological responses of the human body as well as other living things.

That the human being generates and transmits this only partially known energy force has been demonstrated in the study of bioelectrics, acupuncture, and high-frequency photography, and through the use of subtle energy-field detectors. A number of carefully planned investigations have been carried out revealing that healers can transfer a healing force from themselves to another person, that meditation can cure cancer, that thought energy can affect the growth of plants and microscopic life forms.

In all of the above experiments, as well as many psi findings, the human element is an integral quality.

With our pyramid research we can never be sure to what extent we influence the results. We have made every effort to eliminate ourselves as a factor. Where possible we have carried out blind studies, all of which will be described later, but the mind has strange channels in which it moves. Too many studies have demonstrated that distance has little bearing on the effectiveness of psychic or mental energy for us to imagine for a moment that our mere absence from the experimental room dismisses us as a factor.

How can we say that plants behave in a certain way or that milk doesn't sour because of pyramid energy? All we can really report is that unusual phenomena apparently occur in pyramid replicas correctly constructed and oriented to the north-south axis. In the months and years ahead, hopefully, we will learn more about energy fields and the source and nature of the various fields involved.

In the following pages we will describe these phenomena, particularly as they apply to the human being and other living things. We will discuss some of the cases and experiences and will offer some theoretical bases for these occurrences in the light of both scientific knowledge and as understood by the mystical tradition. We believe you will find yourself engrossed in an adventure as awesome as man himself. And we feel reasonably certain that along the way you will discover new dimensions of your own being.

What is so fascinating about sharpening razor blades or preserving grapes? This is a matter for speculation, for either phenomenon has many practical applications. But beyond these possibilities the implications for self-growth are immense. In order to determine why a phenomenon occurs in the manner that it does, one must learn something about energy fields, electromagnetic forces, gamma and cosmic rays, a bit about the chemistry of liquids, the structure of metals . . . horizons widen, wheels start turning.

Pyramids have a habit of leading us on. When you imagine that you have nailed down a fact, the next experiment may produce a different result. In order to learn why, you need new information and another search begins. This occurred when an American and Egyptian team of scientists recently tried to sound the Great Pyramid to determine the location of undiscovered rooms. The computer readouts varied from one day to the next and the investigation was abandoned at least temporarily. New knowledge was required. Did they learn anything about the pyramid? Perhaps not, except to confirm an age-old legend that the structure was an enigma. Yet they undoubtedly learned something about physics, about their instruments, and about themselves.

It occurred with us when, after observing plant movement within pyramid space by means of time-lapse photography, the plants suddenly changed their two-year pattern of moving from west to east and started moving north-south. We had to review our work, take a look at environmental factors, study solar-flare and sunspot activity charts and examine weather cycles. The pyramids had forced upon us the need for new knowledge.

While phenomena occurring inside the pyramid are different from those outside and while some developments are reasonably stable, there is always a sufficient element of the unknown present that the researcher can never complacently contend that he has learned all there is to know. That seems to be the history of the pyramids—they relinquish their secrets slowly, as if by design man must grow in order to understand their meaning. One wonders if the ancient builders hid their secrets so cleverly in order to demand of future investigators an ever-expanding knowledge of their universe and themselves. "Man, know thyself," the Delphic Oracle proclaimed, and when Paul Brunton stayed overnight in the Great Pyramid and was visited by a spirit priest he was told that the real secrets of the pyramids rested within himself.

We have mentioned energy fields. In the following pages, we will be saying a great deal about this subject, hoping to throw a little light on some unknowns and thereby stimulating others to become involved in a fascinating adventure.

Energy itself is an enigma. What is it really?

Until recent years physicists held to the theory that the substance of the universe consisted of particles. The world was made up of objects, things; the world was a noun. Then closer and closer examination uncovered smaller and smaller particles of matter, until they seemed to disappear into energy fields. Substance was not stable, but flux, change, movement. The universe was not a conglomeration of small and large objects, it was not a thing but a becoming; the world was a verb. Now some scientists are saying that under close scrutiny energy fades into consciousness; the world is really a thought.

Space-time is a construct of the human intellect. The German philosopher Immanuel Kant and the astronomer James Jeans said that the universe looks less and less like a big machine and more and more like a great thought.

In the foreword to *Space, Time and Beyond,* Bob Toben states:

"Consciousness is the totality beyond space-time—what may in essence be the real 'I.' We have come to know that consciousness and energy are one; that all of space-time is constructed by consciousness; that our normal perception of reality is a composite of an indefinite number of universes in which we coexist; and that what we perceive as ourselves is only the localized projection of our true selves.

"Therefore our full energies are devoted to the study of consciousness. There is no other task. Working toward a transformation in consciousness is the only game in town.

"The scientific community is exploding with incredible new theories of other space-time possibilities, fundamental energies, self-organizing biogravitational fields, the relation of consciousness to gravity, and consciousness as the missing hidden variable in the structuring of matter . . .

"All over the world phenomena are occurring that cannot be explained within existing belief systems. They are being dismissed and their observers are being called lunatics.

"However, if we properly interpret some of the existing accepted scientific theory, we find that explanations do exist. A new overview, already developing, is replacing those that are dissolving . . . As awareness expands, new tools will develop which, in turn, will be replaced by others. All there is is change.

"Belief systems are now being defined in the language of physics and other sciences. But science is not saying anything new. It is simply restating those views that were understood in different words and symbols thousands of years ago."

If consciousness is the only game in town and this was understood by the ancient architects, as Toben suggests, then one could infer that this was the ultimate message they hoped to relay to us.

It appears that if such is the case, we have come to this knowledge through the exploration of the Great Pyramid by the same circuitous path as physics has moved from matter to mind. From the pyramid we learned a great deal about mechanics, mathematics, and structure. It taught us how to examine the physical nature of our universe. With the discovery that the space inside a pyramid structure produces different phenomena from the space outside it, we are learning more about energy fields. And now in dangling the carrot of elusive energy fields in front of us the pyramids are demanding a greater knowledge of the nature of reality before unveiling all of the particulars to us. It seems evident now that we will be unable to fully comprehend the mysteries of the physical pyramids until we fathom the invisible pyramids within ourselves. A journey, then, must be undertaken . . . and the Gizeh plain beckons us less than the journey inward.

2

Journey to the Center of the Self

"I can't describe it . . . how can I call it a 'loud quiet,' but that is the image which keeps coming to mind."

The 26-year-old woman, who holds a responsible position as a hospital employee, sat in Tom Garrett's living room in Oklahoma City trying to relate to him what she had felt upon her first exposure inside a pyramid.

Garrett, who became enthusiastic about pyramids after several interesting encounters with ours, had constructed a six-foot-tall pyramid and asked friends to spend a short period of time inside. They were told to meditate or simply sit inside for a while—usually twenty to thirty minutes—and to then tell him what they felt, if anything. He made no further suggestions and they were not told the reactions of others until after they related their own experiences. Garrett kept a log on these people for us but as most of the reports had to do with health, dreams, and hypnagogic imagery produced in the twilight zone between waking and sleeping, the experiences will be described in later chapters.

"I was suspended, Tom. I was drawn toward the center

and held there by a comfortable but firm force. A kind of kaleidoscope type of energy was all around me. I felt relaxed and my thought patterns were better organized than I can ever remember their being. I was not alone inside that pyramid . . . I am not sure what I mean by that . . . I was not aware of anyone else, not in the ordinary sense, anyway . . . but a presence, a kind of benevolent force protecting and guiding me. I felt compelled to meditate and it was so easy—the world far away—but always I was aware of the loud quiet, a kind of white noise, if that makes any sense . . ."

The glow in the fireplace had borrowed some fragment of reality from another world as though the fire spirits had gathered therein for some special festivity. Or perhaps it was the breaths of mountain devas whistling through the giant spruces and blowing selected gusts down the chimney that made the fire dance so delightfully.

I closed my eyelids to very narrow slits and used the glow of a single red coal as a mandala for my meditation. Beside me the voice of our Indian instructor was softly saying, "There is a silence that is so deep that it is loud and you can go there . . . and being there you will sometime discover a white fountain, radiant in its light, and you must always move toward the white fountain."

Doors into the twilight zone? What is reality? What is sanity, for that matter, or hallucination or imagination or extrasensory perception? What kind of reality is it that we have in mind? Is my reality of a traffic sign any more substantial than a clairvoyant's vision of a car accident she is able to prevent by giving a warning? It likely depends upon their context and application. Is van Gogh's painting of trees vibrant with whirling energy any less a painting than Renoir's flowers simply because he added a dimension of life that some viewers cannot see?

The new physics has made us realize that reality is not a thing or things correctly perceived but states of awareness sufficiently pragmatic that they can be shared with others in some meaningful fashion. The schizophrenic gets spaced out, not because what he experiences has no basis for existence, but because he finds no way to relate the experience to a set of conditions previously subscribed to by himself and others in his life-space. Better communication between individuals having psychic experiences, the mass media relating of these experiences to the public, scientific confirmation of the reality of psychic activities, and the growth of training principles to develop the extra talents latent in most people have substantially contributed in recent years to a widely held concept that man's five senses alone provide him with a minute and fragmented vision of total reality.

On this the eminent Cambridge philosopher Dr. C. D. Brood once stated, "The function of the brain and nervous system is to protect us from being overwhelmed and confused by this mass of largely useless and irrelevant knowledge, by shutting out most of what we should otherwise perceive or remember at any moment, and leaving only that very small and special selection which is likely to be practically useful."

Thor Myers, a retired Denver bus driver, lay down on the floor and stretched his arms out in cross fashion. "This is the way I lie in my pyramid," he said. "I have a cot that I lie on and some stands beside the cot at the same level so that I can rest my arms on them when they are stretched out. My head is to the north." He closed his eyes and for a moment was silent. The moment stretched into several minutes and we had about decided that he was meditating, but then he said, "I discovered that in this position I feel as though I am being charged with energy. I have meditated for many years and I have some biofeedback equipment but I never experienced before what I have since using the pyramid."

Myers sat up and glanced about the room. He looked at us and shook his head. "I read your book and I knew somehow within myself that this was what I was seeking. This may be difficult to believe, but since I started using the pyramid, information has come to me about many things such as the inner workings of the body, nervous system, and brain. I knew nothing about these things so I started reading in order to confirm what came to me. It has been all true as far as I can tell."

"You would have appeared to have tapped higher levels of consciousness."

"Yes, I think I have."

"Perhaps the pyramid had little to do with this. You mentioned that you had meditated for many years. Maybe these experiences are finally an outcome of your work?"

"Well, it's possible," Myers said slowly, "and it may be that there has been a building up to this point, but I would say that it would more likely be fields of energy or consciousness I've tapped while inside the pyramid." He was thoughtful for a moment and added, "Another reason I believe the pyramid has something to do with it is that it only happens when I meditate inside the pyramid."

Thor Myers is just one of many people we have visited with, or who have called or written to us about their experiences sitting, lying down, sleeping, and meditating inside a pyramid. Of course, we are not likely to hear from those who have experienced little or nothing. Nor are we likely to hear again from the schoolteacher who told us that just being inside a six-foot plastic pyramid for a few minutes made him nervous and depressed.

But we believe that the number of persons who have spent any time at all inside a pyramid and felt nothing at all different is comparatively small. This is not an affirmation of faith or myopia on our part. This conclusion is based on our experiences with asking people to spend some time inside a pyramid and to give us feedback. We have offered little in the way of instructions beyond suggesting that they might wish to sit quietly or lie down or, if they liked, to meditate. With very few exceptions, they experienced the pyramid as a new kind of space in some fashion or another. Other researchers have reported very similar findings. Many of these subjects were not familiar with our work, nor had they read the literature on pyramid research.

To be objective, however, it is important to recognize that the very act of entering an unusual construction such as a pyramid implies that something is supposed to happen. This establishes an attitude of expectation. They will likely be more aware of reactions and more sensitive to both external stimuli and internal states. If this is all that transpires, the pyramid would still be useful as a kind of centering device through which the subject could develop sensitivity and focus awareness.

Many meditation techniques make use of what is known as seed meditation. An object such as a flowerbud, candle flame, or religious symbol is used on which to focus one's attention. The object is to so concentrate on the object that no other thoughts occur. This brings about a singleness of mind and prepares one for mentally moving beyond the object into a nonthinking state in which the intuitive and higher levels of the mind can function. In biofeedback language this would mean moving from a beta state, where there are many thoughts, to alpha, a more relaxed state where the subject becomes engrossed in the thought or problem and less aware of themselves and the world, and thence to theta, where the world disappears and one's mind is enveloped in intuitive flights. The Zen meditator may "watch his breath," and the Yoga practitioner may stare at the tip of his nose, but the seed or focusing object does not have to be of a visual nature. Some people find it easier to concentrate on musical notes or to use a mantram or a simple chant which they repeat over and over again.

It is possible that the pyramid could be used somewhat in the above manner. Perhaps this could be done by simply being mentally occupied with the thought of the pyramid. Yet, it would be extremely difficult to keep this thought in a singular mental form. More than likely an individual would think about all the things a pyramid was supposed to do or, if they knew nothing about pyramids, to sit and wonder about it and to ask themselves myriad questions as to why they were asked to do this.

The subjective experiences could be simply a matter of imagination. But then, Einstein said, "Imagination is more important than knowledge," and Richard Feynman once stated, "What we need is imagination. We have to find a new view of the world." And this latter statement suggests that new horizons cannot be charted without imagination. Well and good, but our question as to whether reactions to pyramid space are only imagination and therefore could as easily occur outside as inside cannot be answered with a simple yes or no.

It is probably safe to say that imagination plays some integral role in all our mental activities. However, the products of our imaginations are usually uniquely personal in nature. We borrow from our unconscious and conscious minds, along with some unknown input from the superconscious, and build our own little constructs. The feedback we have received from subjects experiencing pyramid space, on the other hand, has many common denominators. This suggests a common or shared resource of influence or information, such as the following:

1. The experiences to some extent are new and usually a little puzzling to the subjects.

2. There is a feeling of isolation, not uncomfortable but rather pleasant, in which the subjects experience peace and quietude. Although conscious of the fact that the composition of the pyramid—plastic, wood, or whatever—is such that they are not physically cut off from street sounds or persons talking in nearby rooms, nevertheless the sensation persists that they have entered their own secluded world. The subjects will sometimes compare the feeling to being deep in the woods or beside a still lake alone. Noises are still heard, vibrations are still felt, but are experienced in a removed, secondary fashion.

3. A sense of security or protection takes over when they enter the pyramid. They will even reason that there is nothing about the pyramid that can protect them from whatever there is that might threaten them. Yet this sense of being guarded remains. This summer a group of us held a meditation retreat in the Colorado mountains. We constructed a plastic pyramid large enough to sleep in and each took a turn of sleeping one night in it. It was somewhat removed from the main lodge in a clearing surrounded by trees and a flashlight was required to find it in

the dark. Two female members of the group stated later that they felt uneasy and a little frightened on their way alone to the pyramid but upon stepping inside the pyramid all fear and anxiety were dissipated.

4. A time-warp is a common experience. Whether the length of stay is an hour or all night, time becomes very distorted. Sometimes the subject will believe he has been inside much longer than he has and other times the experience will be the reverse, but a true evaluation of time is seldom experienced.

5. Sleep inside the pyramid seems to be somehow intensified. Oftentimes persons who have taken short naps will report feeling as rested as if they had slept many hours. During our Colorado experiences several participants stated that they slept very few hours inside the pyramid—going to bed late, getting up very early, and lying awake studying the night sky—yet felt completely rested when they awoke and vigorous throughout the day.

6. Although there is a feeling of being alone inside the pyramid, there is also, concurrently, the sensation of a presence. This does not seem to take on the characteristics of a personality or a disincarnate spirit but there is an awareness of being, sometimes likened to a guardian angel.

7. Meditation is reportedly easier inside the pyramid. Perhaps this is partly the result of feeling isolated from distractions. Those who do not meditate report finding it easy to relax. One of our friends uses the pyramid as a place in which to concentrate on his studies. One person, trying the pyramid for the first time, reported feeling as though he wanted to meditate even though he had never done so.

8. Dreams are reported as being quite vivid, sometimes better organized or understandable, and can be more easily recalled after waking.

9. Hypnagogic imagery—visual images, scenes, sometimes answers to long-standing problems, and occasionally completely new insights that occur just before falling off to sleep—are reportedly more vivid and the period of the imagery seems to last a longer period of time.

10. An awareness of peace seems to come to many who spend any time at all inside pyramids. They find it difficult to harbor feelings of hostility and anger seems to fade away. One person told us that feeling a great peace settling over him he tried to think of all the tension and problems of the world only to discover that he could not retain these thoughts. Another person left her office quite upset over some problems and found that by the time she emerged from the pyramid, approximately an hour later, she could hardly remember what the problems were.

11. An awareness of the presence of an unusual energy field is experienced by perhaps half of the subjects. They sense it more in the middle of the pyramid than elsewhere and feel they are vitalized by it. The C.J.F. family of Oklahoma City, Oklahoma, wrote us a note stating, "Dr. J.K. told us over the phone which direction each member of the family should face when sitting in or meditating. Seems to be correct for each member. The direction matches the direction that a psychic on the west coast said my vibrations went, which is south . . . When falling asleep, the sleep is deep. None of our family has been in longer than one hour yet. The feeling of having been asleep seems to stay with you for quite a while."

12. Several subjects have reported a growing sense of oneness with all life the longer they remain inside the pyramid.

As to why the teacher, mentioned earlier in this chapter, felt nervous and depressed after a short duration inside one of our pyramids we are not sure. We might speculate that he brought these feelings with him and they were intensified by the pyramid's energy field. We might also venture that the pyramid can serve to mirror oneself and this is oppressive to some people. Or perhaps the growth and insight gained by some people inside pyramids serves as a threat to others. We are not certain, of course, that it is any of these things. This, again, is another area where much research has to be done. We can only say at this time that our experiences and that of others, with few exceptions, have been beneficial and meaningful. If, by chance, one does experience an uncomfortable or distressing sensation or thought, it might be wise to leave the pyramid, at least for the time being.

A number of the experiences, feelings, sensations, and so on described above will be discussed at some length later in the book in order to shed as much scientific light as possible on them. Where these experiences occur in other settings and as results of other conditions, efforts will be made to extract the common denominators so that we can better understand the causes and effects involved.

The fact that many of these experiences were unique and occurring with many subjects for the first time suggests a new sensitivity or shift in consciousness. It may be too much to ask if they will ever be the same again or ever hope to be, but that some metamorphosis occurred, however permanent or transient it may be, warrants further investigation.

Most scientists now agree that the brain and the mind are not one and the same thing. Consciousness as such cannot be found within the cells of the organic brain. The electrochemical network and nerve responses in the brain can be mapped by medical scientists. Consciousness itself, however, escapes them. There exists within the cranium a whole world of forces—forces within forces, exceeding any other cubic half-foot of the universe.

Subnuclear particles, neutrons, protons, molecules, cells, and so on have little to say, so it seems, as to what goes on in the brain. These physical components apparently only carry out orders from a higher command.

Somewhere toward the apex of the brain's command system we discover ideas. An idea claims as great a reality as that of a molecule or cell, for ideas create ideas. They not only interact with each other, but also with other mental forces in the same brain, and with the brains of other persons. Further, they apparently have influence on external surroundings.

There is sufficient evidence to indicate that the will-o'-the-wisp energy force of consciousness does interact with the energy forces of the brain and nervous system. A hypothesis can be drawn that the energy fields are one and the same and that the nature of their substance depends upon the perceptivity of the recorder, whether this is a machine or a human observer. This approach parallels that of occult physics, which holds to a concept of energy and a related field theory that there is one primary form of energy out of which everything is constructed.

Study of this singular energy force is underway in a number of laboratories in this and other countries. It is believed that an understanding of the laws governing this force will provide explanations of various psychic phenomena which to date have eluded hard-data scientific investigations.

These energy fields were discussed in *The Secret Power of Pyramids* and will be discussed further in later chapters. The nature of energy and consciousness and to what extent they coexist as expressions of a singular force will likely have considerable importance on our understanding of what happens to a person's feelings and thoughts while inside a pyramid. The links between matter and energy, and energy and consciousness, when understood, should provide a bridge to move easily from one realm to another. Further, we may learn how form can change energy fields and how mental forms can generate energy. The pyramid may serve as the bridge between these worlds.

Consciousness as a "thing," an object, or as an experience, is difficult to define except in a circular fashion such as Dr. Annie Besant used in *A Study in Consciousness:* "Consciousness and life are identical . . . we have called consciousness turned inwards by the name of life, and life turned outwards by the name of consciousness." In *The Secret Doctrine,* H. P. Blavatsky refers to consciousness as the finest and loftiest form of energy, the root of all things, and coextensive with cosmic space. In this model, consciousness and matter are not to be regarded as independent realities but as aspects of a single reality.

In *The Phenomenon of Man,* Pierre Teilhard de Chardin noted that "from the phenomenal point of view, matter and spirit do not present themselves as 'things' or 'natures' but as simple related variables."

While brain and mind can be seen as different expressions of the same singular force, in order to examine the shifts in consciousness experienced by persons sitting and meditating inside pyramids, some further division needs to be drawn. Apparently these experiences occur when attention has moved from the reasoning or cognitive process to intuitive levels. When this occurs, information coming into the awareness is not the product of reasoning but comes from a source outside of or beyond the rational mind.

Intuition does not contradict reason, Swami Vishnudevananda claims in *The Complete Book of Yoga,* "but transcends reason and brings knowledge and wisdom from its field of consciousness, which the intellect cannot penetrate . . . Reason helps us to march to the door of intuition. Reason can give us the information that the experiences of the phenomenal world are unreal when compared with the everlasting experiences of self-realization. Reason has its own definite utility as it helps in the beginning when we start the quest of truth."

Alexander Maven spoke of the elements of intuitive levels of the mind:

"Mystics are almost unanimous in saying that the experience is more immediate than any ordinary experience, so immediate that its reality cannot be doubted. Some even have said the reality disclosed by mystical experience is the only reality, all else being illusion. Their awareness of the experience has been said to be beyond sensing, perceiving, conceptualizing, reasoning, or understanding and unlike anything remembered or imagined. It is, the mystics say, pure intuition, pure consciousness. All this seems tantamount to saying that the awareness is beyond the functioning of a nervous system and a brain . . ."

The altered states of consciousness, the greater sensitivity, the distortion of time, the feeling of a flow of energy, the visual observations, the dissociation from the external world, and other paranormal experiences of persons spending time inside pyramids might best be described as a shift from the left to the right hemisphere of the brain. While this is an assumption, the kind of subjective experiences reported would seem to indicate more right than left hemisphere activity.

The left hemisphere of the brain is associated more with the reasoning process and the right hemisphere is identified with the intuition. Perhaps when a person steps into a pyramid, he is confronted with an illogical set of conditions. There is nothing about the pyramid that attracts the attention of his senses, nor the presence of anything with which he can deal rationally. In order to cope with his experience, he unconsciously shifts from the left to the right hemisphere activity. When a person contacts the intuitive mind, he experiences himself and his environment in a different way. As with high meditation and mystical states, his experiences are ineffable, that is, he cannot find words to express his thoughts and feelings. This is understandable, as language is primarily a function of the left hemisphere of the brain.

In a sense, one can describe the initial goal of meditation and some Yoga exercises to be to shift from the rational arena of the left hemisphere to the artistic, creative, and intuitive flights of the right hemisphere. This is also one of the goals in biofeedback training: to move the brainwaves from the stimuli-responding beta state to the contemplative level of the theta state.

". . . Move toward the white fountain . . . ," our teacher said. Perhaps the pyramid will help show us the way.

3

The Psychic Unfoldment

A universe of whirling, flowing energies, the matrix of all things, coming from, existing within one single unified force—this is the substance of the new physics.

"All things are interconnected . . . Every part of your universe is directly connected to every other part . . . The description of any part is inseparable from the description of the whole . . . You cannot move without influencing everything in your universe . . . You cannot even observe anything without changing the object and even yourself . . . It is even possible that just thinking about an object can change it and yourself . . . All the universe is alive . . . All the universe is interconnected . . . There is life in everything but with varying degrees of consciousness . . ." The aphorisms of Bob Toben are an experience in reading. His book *Space, Time and Beyond* was written from conversations with physicists Jack Sarfatti and Fred Wolf, and not too many years ago we would have accused him of carrying on a dialogue with wild-eyed science-fiction writers, or we might simply have called him a poet. But today Bob Toben is a scientist, a perceptive one, and his conversants, both holding doctorate degrees in physics and responsible faculty positions, have their credentials well in order.

When Toben states, "Consciousness and energy are one," he is echoed by Sarfatti saying, "I suspect that general relativity and quantum theory are simply two complementary aspects of a deeper theory that will involve a kind of cosmic consciousness as the key concept."

A pyramid that is alive? Obviously, such an idea must be rejected or, if we hope to cope with it, we must struggle to establish some new reality bases. On the one hand we have a box, not dissimilar from any other box except that it has triangular sides that come together at a point. It has no other notable distinctions and is made from almost anything; if it claims any peculiarities of its own, they are simply that it must be constructed according to a certain pattern and must be placed in a particular position. On the other hand, we have an instrument that performs a multitude of tasks, not all of which appear directly related, and its modus operandi demands the best of our knowledge in many fields. As the nondescript box and the highly complex instrument are one and the same, how do we resolve the riddle?

The new physics may help. It tells us that particles or objects as such do not exist but that everything in the universe is energy. Objects or things are only mental structures and have form only so long as they are observed as such. But we then discover that the closer we examine energy the more readily it disappears into consciousness, and here we are with our thoughts examining thoughts. On the one hand the world still exists if we can accept it as an effect and not a cause, but we have lost the world as a collection of objects, of big and small things.

In many ways we are not prepared to deal with a world as a thought. It is too great a step to jump from object to subject. We need to build a bridge between the world of things and the world of ideas. We need to live in an intermediary world for a while to make the adjustment. This resting place can be reasonably well provided for a time by the island of energy. In this place we no longer experience form; instead we experience change. Our experiences are not with things, not with items having dimensions, but with flow, with movement. We have not reached that point where we are ready to excuse space and time as only thought creations, so we still speak of "things" such as wavelengths and energy fields, and sparks and lights, and so on, because we still insist on nouns. But now instead of trying to understand them as sitting still, we try to perceive them as a collection of very small units in rapid motion. We try to look behind to see what is going on instead of accepting outward appearance.

"I like to sit in parks and bus depots and watch. Real people look like luminous eggs when you see them," Don Juan tells Carlos Castaneda in describing ordinary looking and real "seeing." The Yaqui Indian explains that sometimes in a crowd of egglike creatures he notices one who looks exactly like a person, and then he knows that there is something wrong and that, without the luminous glow, this is not a real person at all.

"How long I had been sitting in my pyramid I do not know. I lost track of time. I may have fallen asleep, but then I was conscious of myself sitting there and as I looked out from somewhere inside myself there was the realization that the pyramid was on fire, the whole structure was outlined in small tonguelike flames. For some reason I wasn't alarmed, nor did I try to move. I sat there awed by what I saw. The flames died out and I couldn't see the pyramid at all but I had the strangest sensation that it was extended a long, long way from me in every direction."

In order to grasp the meaning of the pyramid we find that we progress very little in treating it as an object. As the artist must become one with his brushes, his paint, and his canvas in order to truly paint, so we have learned that we must interact with the pyramid to be able to move beyond the structure to the phenomena itself. When we relate to the pyramid as an energy field, we discover it has much in common with ourselves.

When clairvoyants look at a pyramid they see a radiant,

changing field of light. Inanimate objects—cardboard, wood, tape, the materials that pyramids are made of—do not glow in this manner. Put together in the correct fashion these inactive substances become some kind of living force, one that our perceptive friends tell us emulates in many ways the human structure.

Another fascinating parallel can be drawn. The phenomena produced by pyramids resemble very closely that produced by some talented persons. We mentioned in *The Secret Power of Pyramids* that when our psychic friend Charles Rhoades learned we were keeping razor blades sharp in pyramids he challenged us that he would keep his blade sharp just by running his fingers over it each day. Two years later he was still faithful to the same blade. Persons who have gained considerable control over their physical, emotional, and mental states are oftentimes able to influence tranquillity, sensitivity, and elevated states of awareness in others. Accomplished healers such as Olga Worrall and Oskar Estebany have been able to treat water, preserve food items, stimulate the growth of plants, and bring about healing in many ways similar to those seemingly produced by pyramids.

It is doubtful whether many of us would be able to select from a crowd those who are healers, clairvoyants, or persons with unusual psychic abilities. As far as their physical appearance is concerned, they look like any other members of the human race. But put them on biofeedback monitoring devices, scan them with sensitive energy-field detectors, or take Kirlian photographs of their fingerpads in performance of their talents and different profiles emerge than with average persons.

It would seem that persons with extra talents are attuned to a universal source of energy and consciousness and their auras are all aglow much as a pyramid built and aligned correctly is charged with energy. But the average person, like a pyramid out of alignment, fails to radiate this magnitude of light.

Buckminster Fuller points out that ninety-nine percent of what is happening in human activity and interaction within nature takes place in realms of reality utterly invisible, inaudible, unsmellable, untouchable by presently developed human senses and must be relayed to us by instruments. Fortunately, most scholars in the field of paranormal powers agree that these skills are present in a latent state in everyone, waiting to be developed by the proper education and techniques.

What is happening within, or even perhaps near, the pyramid remains beyond the level of average human perception. Much of this activity also lies outside the detection of our most sophisticated instruments; the gap is being closed somewhat, however, thanks to the technological advances of recent years. Techniques for measuring energy fields in and around pyramids are discussed in a later chapter. While these are far from conclusive, they do provide some insights and sufficient evidence to lead us to propose that additional hard data on pyramid energy fields are not too far around the corner. But there does seem to be the need to bear in mind that some of this phenomena, while producing tangible results and influencing states of awareness, will never be detectable by physical instruments since it is not of a physical nature. Just as a brainwave is detectable on an electroencephalograph, the idea enshrouded within the brainwave forever eludes us.

There is a level just beyond the dense physical one, however, that can be examined and can provide us with some insight into a portion of pyramid phenomena and human phenomena as well. This is the dimension of electricity, gravity, magnetism, electromagnetic forces, radio waves, cosmic rays, and so on. As these fields apply to the human body, they are oftentimes referred to as auric, etheric, or simply bioelectrical. This is not to say, however, that these fields are identical even though to the untrained observer they may appear so. On the other hand, the most highly trained scientist may find himself working with phenomena that he finds difficult to classify. Using his instruments, he may attempt to define his findings as being the same as those reported by the clairvoyant, using only his own powers of perception. These observations do not always closely correspond, however, even though the superficial phenomena have similar qualities. This is presently occurring in the investigation of acupuncture where efforts to identify acupuncture meridians as being directly related to nerve current haven't jelled. This problem in identification is also happening in the exploration of high-frequency photography (the Kirlian technique). Some researchers have attempted to identify the electrical discharges around animate objects, particularly the human body, as being the same as the aura seen by clairvoyants. Other researchers claim the field is merely an electrical artifact, while the clairvoyant is saying to both camps that Kirlian photographs reveal only a small portion and limited properties of the aura.

The evidence indicates that part of pyramid phenomena lies within the etheric spectrum. As mentioned earlier, the etheric is seen as the level just above or slightly less dense than physical matter. According to the mystical tradition, all disease, mental disturbance, distress, and so forth must first occur within the etheric envelope or vital sheath before it becomes materialized in the physical body. This model is developed further in the chapters on "The Healing Phenomenon." It might also be noted here that one of the uses now being explored for Kirlian photography is to take a picture of the electrical field around the body and thereby detect disease before it becomes manifest in the body. Research on this to date would indicate the method will become a valuable diagnostic aid.

It would seem that it is at the etheric level that the human being interacts with the pyramid. Interaction may also occur, of course, at levels above the etheric, but it is this level that we are concerned with here. Since it is obvious that the pyramid does not affect the body by way of administering pills, performing surgery, or other physical acts, we must explore the interaction at the next closest level.

Within the mystical tradition, physical matter exists in seven grades of density: atomic, subatomic, superetheric, etheric, gaseous, liquid, and solid. Particles of all these grades enter into the composition of the physical body. The latter, however, has two well-marked divisions: the dense body, composed of solids, liquids, and gases, and the etheric, consisting of the finer grades of physical matter.

According to this tradition, the etheric envelope performs a number of roles, including the following: it receives and distributes the vital force that emanates from the sun and is thus intimately connected with physical health; upon the action of etheric matter mainly depends the memory of the dream life; it is especially associated with what is known as vital or magnetic healing, whether for purposes of healing, anesthesia or trance; it is the principal factor in psi phenomenon such as the movement of objects without physical force, production of sounds, telepathy, psychometry, and so on; and by use of the matter of the etheric body, objects may be magnetized.

Every solid, liquid, and gaseous particle of the physical body is surrounded with an etheric envelope, according to this model. There are four grades of etheric matter and their properties and functions are: (1) etheric—the medium of ordinary current electricity and of sound; (2) superetheric—the medium of light; (3) subatomic—the medium of finer forms of electricity; (4) atomic—the medium for the transmission of thought from brain to brain.

Mystical Tradition	Physics	Example
E_1 Atomic	Electronic	Electron
E_2 Subatomic	Positive Nucleus	Alpha Particle
E_3 Superetheric	Neutralized Nucleus	Neutron
E_4 Etheric	Atomic	Nascent N
Gaseous	Molecular gas, etc.	Atomic H
		H_2, N_2, or gaseous compounds

In appearance the etheric body or double is a pale violet, gray or blue-gray, faintly luminous, and coarse or fine in texture according as the physical body is coarse or fine. This has been observed by several persons with some psychic sensitivity. Some have claimed seeing a blue halo around the Great Pyramid.

"I wouldn't want to imply that I always see lights around pyramids," Mrs. C.D. of Dallas, Texas, wrote us, "but on occasion, perhaps when the light is just right, I see a blue glow around the entire pyramid. It is particularly bright at the apex where it sometimes looks violet in color."

The etheric envelope allegedly acts as an intermediary or bridge between the dense physical body and the astral (emotional-mental) body, transmitting the consciousness of physical sense contacts through the etheric brain to the astral body, and also transmitting consciousness from the astral and higher levels down into the physical brain and nervous system.

The etheric is the integrating energy that coordinates the physical molecules, cells, and so on, and holds them together as a definite organism. According to the mystical tradition, were it not for the presence of prana, there could be no physical body as an integral whole; without the etheric envelope the body would be nothing more than a collection of independent cells. On the physical plane the etheric energy builds up all minerals, and is the controlling agent in the chemicophysiological changes in protoplasm, which lead to differentiation and the building of the various tissues of the bodies of plants, animals, and men. The blending of the astral—the emotional-mental substance above the etheric—with the etheric creates nerve matter, which is fundamentally the cell, and which gives the power to feel pleasure and pain. The cells develop into fibers, as result of thought, the etheric pulsating along the fibers being composed of physical, emotional, and mental energy.

According to this model, there appears first in the astral body a center, having the function of receiving and responding to vibrations from outside. From this center, vibrations pass to the etheric body, causing there etheric vortices which draw into themselves dense physical particles; these eventually form a nerve cell, and groups of cells which, receiving vibrations from the outer physical world, transmit them back to the astral centers, the physical and astral centers thus acting and reacting on one another, each in consequence becoming more complicated and more effective. Out of these nerve cells the sympathetic system is built first, by impulses, as described, originating on the astral level; later the cerebrospinal system is constructed by impulse originating in the mental world. From the centers the sense centers in the brain are formed, five connected with eyes, ears, tongue, nose, and skin, and five to convey vibrations from consciousness to the outer world.

Etheric energy, or prana, as it is sometimes called, which courses along the nerves, is believed to be separate and distinct from what is called a person's magnetism, or nerve fluid, which is generated within the body. The nerve fluid or magnetism keeps the etheric matter circulating along the nerves, much as the blood circulates through the veins. And just as the blood carries oxygen to the body, so does the nerve fluid convey prana or etheric energy.

The above description of the manner in which etheric energy functions in the human body will serve its turn in the following chapter when we discuss how the pyramid appears to influence the activation of energy systems in the body leading to psychic development and higher states of consciousness. It will also be of value when we consider the process of healing and how forces generated or amplified by pyramids tend to quicken this process. The mystical model has been used for the reason that at this point in our understanding it better explains the seeming interaction between pyramid forces and the human system. In recent years the mystical model of the human system—developed for the most part in Eastern psychological and physiological philosophies—and the scientific model have moved much closer together. While the language is to some extent different, the principles appear to be on converging paths. This is partly due, at least, to the development of sensitive monitoring devices which allow us to explore dimensions of man and his universe heretofore out of reach of traditional scientific examination. We believe the pyramid, as an instrument generating or amplifying these subtle fields, will make a contribution to this exploration.

These vital energy fields in man and his universe are described in a recent paper, "The Energy Field of Man," by Dr. John Pierrakos, a New York psychiatrist. These inner pulsatory movements, he states, "are the sum total of the processes of life: of all the energies of the metabolism of life within his body. This sum total of energies within his body, also flows out of his body, in the same manner as a heat wave travels out of an incandescent metal object. They create an energy field made up of lines of force in the periphery of his organism. Man's body lives within this energy field which extends several feet away in the immediate vicinity, and at times can be seen traveling several dozen feet out of himself."

Later in the same paper Dr. Pierrakos states, "This phenomena constitutes the energy field, or Aura, which is, in effect a reflection of the energies of life processes . . . The Aura, or energy field, is a light cast of the body energies . . . The field phenomena belong, in addition, to another dimension. They are energetic phenomena that transcend the physical realities of matter and, even though they are tied up with the structure and matter of the body, they have their own laws of pulsatory movement and vibration not yet understood."

The nature of the aura or etheric energy has a long history of description by mystics. During the last century, however, Baron von Reichenbach made a detailed study of the energy field of crystals, animals, and plants. In this century, Dr. W. J. Kilner investigated the human energy field through the use of colored screens; Dr. Wilhelm Reich demonstrated the existence of the elusive field force by means of amplifying it in a six-sided box he called an "oraccu"; Drs. H. S. Burr and F. S. C. Northrop discussed vital energies as the cohesive force between complex chemical interchanges and biological processes; Dr. Pierrakos used colored glass to make the aura visible; and the latest technique is that of high-frequency photography.

So there have been a variety of efforts to detect and explain these subtle, complex energy fields, whether we call them auras, etheric energies, vital forces, prana, bioplasma, or whatever. With the pyramid we are offered another opportunity of exploring this force field. As the adventure is available to any interested person—and we have been amazed at how quickly this interest has grown—the research is not limited to a handful of scientific examiners and our body of knowledge can be gathered from laboratory, basement, and workshop far and wide. One of the most exciting aspects of this journey is that the experiments can be designed around almost anyone's whims, from the professional researcher measuring minute changes a thousand times to the armchair philosopher who prefers to sit in his pyramid and jot down daydreams in his diary. All whimsies and idiosyncracies are to be valued lest we forget that five hundred years ago a Chinese sage sat under his peach tree, contemplated the moon for a spell, and provided us with its weight, density, and distance from the earth.

It has been necessary in this chapter to explore the different levels of energy. Hopefully, such investigations will help us to understand better what may be happening in pyramid space. It is imperative that all of us continue to think in terms of "may be happening," for it will be some time yet before we can say "this is what is occurring." With this approach, we keep the doors ajar to all possible rooms of knowledge. We must not jump to conclusions just because several respected clairvoyants agree as to their observations or because a couple of scientists produce similar computer readouts. If we rush closure on these matters, we may sacrifice greater for lesser truths. The division of substance from the dense physical to the spiritual provides us a way of looking at pyramid phenomena.

There are reasons to believe that pyramid fields assist in the realization of these extended or higher talents. While this can be all to the good and work toward the benefit of both the individual and the human race, there are some sober matters to consider before launching oneself on this exciting journey. This is primarily true when one thinks of the development of psychic powers.

The development of psychic powers in itself has been considered by the world's great teachers as an endeavor to be avoided. But pick up any magazine on the occult and you can find several dozen self-styled teachers yearning to open the secrets of hidden powers for you—through a set of their books, correspondence course, tapes, classes, a workshop deep in the woods of somewhere, or whatever.

There is nothing wrong with these magazines; we read them, we even write for several of them. They carry some excellent material. There is nothing wrong with the occult —or some of it, anyway. The word refers to that which is hidden, the esoteric. The occult was born of the mystical approach to knowledge in which the information provided was not accessible except to those so talented. The occult certainly has had many followers who have used it for selfish and detrimental purposes; but then, so has science, business, medicine, and politics.

Some of these teachers of the occult have valuable information to pass along to their students, having to do with self-awareness, growth, extending horizons. That some of them really have little to offer, are somewhat spaced-out, or have faulty powers of discrimination and leave their followers a bit worse off than they were before—including financially—doesn't particularly set them apart from any other group—physicians, psychiatrists, brokers, mechanics—with their good guys and bad guys.

Then, what's wrong? Well, to illustrate, if you were to go to certain places in India today you would be besieged by persons representing themselves as yogis who would offer to teach you some magic tricks. They wouldn't call it that—they'd refer to their offerings as "self-mastery," "control of the body and mind," or something similar, and they would even demonstrate some psychic talent which they would assure you could be yours if you placed yourself in their hands for a time. But let's say that you went to India already in possession of some self-awareness and were there with the serious intent of gaining more, you would pass on by. You would know that if they approached you, they would not be the teachers you were in search of. Further, you would know that if they offered you enlightenment, you could rest assured that they couldn't deliver it. And still further, you would know that the teacher you were in search of would be extremely difficult to find, even more difficult to recruit, and once recruited would promise you nothing.

What is the difference between the two types of teachers? Is the one just better and thus can play hard to get? No, the two teachers are poles apart. The one, while he may have a certain degree of psychic ability and perhaps can even teach it, is not an elevated being in any real sense. He is not seeking the unfolding of man's higher being, the expanding of the human potential; he is a peddler seeking survival, fortune, and fame, and his wares are psychic tricks. The other teacher, on the other hand, is seeking the elevation of the human race. Money, fame, or power are of no use to him. He will accept you as a student only because he discovers within you the potentiality for furthering the cause of enlightenment. That you might be a person in a position to make his name known is of no interest to him, and as a matter of fact, if you had the intention of doing this, he would know you were not mature enough to benefit from his teachings. Once accepted as a student, you would likely go through years of training and not once during this time would your teacher have instructed you in the development of your psychic powers. But amazingly enough, when you left him to go out into the world, you would possess considerable psychic skills, and yet, you would neither demonstrate these talents before the public nor would you teach them per se to others. You would use them, of course, in a variety of ways but you would never exhibit them as an isolated phenomenon.

It has been the practice of all great teachers to speak of discovering the inner, the higher self, to elevate the consciousness and find one's spiritual heritage. It is impossible, however, to find in their words or their writings instructions for developing psychic abilities. It is doubtful whether the builders of the Great Pyramid had the unfolding of psychic powers in mind when they undertook their colossal task. If they were the enlightened beings they appear to be, their purposes would have been more elevated than this.

Why are psychic powers a no-no? They aren't. They are to be desired, to be cultivated and protected. But the seers knew, and know, that the human being is so constructed that it is essential that his sights are set unwaveringly on the goal—samadhi, perfection, enlightenment. If he endeavors to use some additional talent obtained somewhere along the path before he gains control over his ego, desires, body, emotions, and mind, and has won the spiritual insight that illuminates his vision, he will not have the selflessness, maturity, and judgment to use this talent with wisdom.

This chapter is not intended to be a lecture on virtue, but it is important to us to make available to the reader some information that could have a profound effect on his life. It would be irresponsible of us to offer an approach that has demonstrated success in expanding human functioning and then avoid what to us seems imperative by way of instruction. Something happens inside the pyramid. We have reason to believe—from personal experiences, letters, phone calls, learning of the findings of other researchers—that the unusual fields inside pyramids may well generate psychic abilities.

"One afternoon while sitting in my pyramid my mind kept repeating an image of a black United Parcel Service truck. I tired of these images and left the pyramid to return to the living room. I no sooner sat down than the doorbell rang and when I opened the door I was shocked to see a United Parcel Service truck in the street in front of my house. The delivery man wanted to leave a package with me for my next-door neighbor who was not home at the time."

"Actually I was just sitting in my pyramid and not even meditating and suddenly I wasn't in my body any longer! Somehow I was outside and was looking at my body sitting inside."

"My friend and I tried sending mental messages to each other over a year ago with little success. Then several weeks ago we both constructed pyramids and tried telepathy while sitting inside of them. Now we're getting through with a few things and it seems to be getting steadily better."

These experiences are not something to be frightened of, or to be necessarily avoided. They can be worthwhile, but any new skill, while a privilege, carries a tremendous responsibility. There is an old saying, "For every step you take toward psychic achievement, take ten steps toward spiritual growth." "So above, so below; so below, so above" is another aphorism of some antiquity and we are all familiar with cases where a newly won talent exercised without an equal gain in self-control and judgment brought downfall and heartache.

We would not place a loaded gun in an infant's hands. A knife in the hand of a skilled surgeon can save lives; it takes life in the hands of an assassin. We would not give the keys of our car to a nondriver, and karate was not meant to be taught to those of violent nature. Psychic skills offer much to those who are prepared to use them for the benefit of themselves and others. But good intentions are not good enough. These skills must be used properly. A well-meaning but untrained cook, after all, can give us ptomaine.

What should we do about pyramid experiments? Pursue them. There is no way of turning off new knowledge, nor is there a need. The benefits of air travel far outdistance the hazards. If our timidity would get the best of us, we would not progress on any front. But pyramid research is no longer fun and games. We are dealing with a real force. It shows promise of being of considerable benefit to us on several fronts and several levels. Yet the gift cannot be accepted without accepting the demands this new knowledge makes on us as responsible human beings. Once again the pyramid had taken us within ourselves where we must examine our motives, our stability, our willingness to grow. We are not comparing pyramid force with nuclear fusion, but the illustration fits well enough when we point to the fact that we developed the atom bomb before we developed a kinship with all of life, and the lesson is clear.

When you saw the title of this chapter in the Table of Contents perhaps you thought, "Great, I'll get some information on how to move physical objects with my hands in my pockets." Instead you ended up with a lecture. Well, the Delphic Oracle said, "Man, know thyself," and when Paul Brunton stayed overnight in the Great Pyramid, he was told by his spiritual mentor that the real knowledge of the pyramid rested within himself. Self-awareness, higher consciousness, is really the only game in town, but we have to play by the rules if we really wish to win.

We have a friend who heard about a chant that was supposed to be particularly effective in materializing physical needs. She needed ten thousand dollars and so she held this sum of money in her mind and did the chant as instructed. Within a short time she received exactly that sum of money, no more and no less. It was awarded to her by the death of her father. She had the need, the tool to supply the need, but not the powers of discrimination that would have allowed her to achieve her goal wisely.

What if the pyramid forces psychic powers upon me? No, this will never happen. That isn't the way the law of attraction works. You draw to yourself what you consciously and unconsciously desire. You are responsible; not something or someone else. The world's great teachers have always told us that we create our world. The pyramid is there. It is a gift. Its secrets have come to us slowly over the centuries, hoping perhaps that we would grow into them. It can do no more; the rest is up to us.

4

The Serpent's Fire

"I had spent the evening in a quiet city with some friends reading and discussing poetry and philosophy. We had regaled ourselves with Wordsworth, Shelley, Browning, and especially Whitman. We parted at midnight. I had a long drive in a hansom to my lodgings. My mind traveled under the influence of the ideas, images and emotions called up by the reading and talking. I was in a state of mind of most peaceful enjoyment, not actually thinking but letting images, ideas and emotions, fleet of themselves, and spread throughout my mind. All at once, without warning of any kind, I found myself wrapped in a coloured cloud. For an instant I thought of fire, an immense conflagration somewhere close by, in that great city. The next moment I knew that the fire was within myself."

The above passage has become a classic in the description of a little-understood phenomenon in man's realization of higher states of being. It is taken from *Cosmic Consciousness,* written by Dr. R. M. Bucke, in which he describes his experiences in a break-through in consciousness, or what is sometimes referred to as the rising of the kundalini—the serpent's fire.

"A great deal of very interesting work is waiting to be done on the kundalini, the psychic or spiritual energy which is said to be in every human body at the base of the spine and which can, under certain circumstances, be aroused so as to irrigate and irradiate consciousness as it mounts up the spine to the brain," Dr. Karan Singh, India's minister of Health and Family Planning, stated during his inaugural address at "The Seminar on Yoga, Science and Man," held in New Delhi on March 14, 1975.

An interesting Egyptian image is the serpent with his tail in his mouth, symbolizing infinity, the unending continuity of life. In the biblical story of Adam and Eve in the Garden of Eden, the serpent offers the fruit of the tree of knowledge. Eating of the fruit, Adam and Eve became self-conscious and are thus separated from the other animals; they are no longer part of the Group Mind and must pay the penalty for individualized consciousness. They are responsible for their acts. But, according to Egyptian mysteries, they can find their way back to the Garden and oneness with Omnipotence through enlightenment. The serpent that was responsible for the exile is also responsible for their return . . . the serpent with his tail in his mouth. The serpent is once again the symbol of enlightenment when we consider the kundalini phenomenon. Allegedly, enlightenment is not possible without experiencing the rising of the kundalini. If the pyramid contributes to this development—to be explored in this chapter—then the Egyptians have provided us not only with the symbol of this occurrence, but an instrument for its achievement as well.

Perhaps the most widely read discussant of the kundalini experience is Gopi Krishna who, after realizing the awakened state, has demonstrated his increased awareness for the benefit of science and has been advocating its more thorough scientific research. He has attracted the attention of a number of eminent Western scientists who are currently endeavoring to develop research plans for the examination of the kundalini phenomenon.

Speaking of Gopi Krishna, D. K. Vyas wrote in the March 29, 1975, edition of *The Hindustan Times:*

"Mr. Gopi Krishna, a yogi from Kashmir, believes that the awakening of 'Kundalini' (the divine power that lies dormant at the base of the spinal cord in the form of a coiled serpent) through yoga or other suitable disciplines produces a 'scientifically measurable biochemical essence that is responsible for the phenomenon of genius as well as for the process of evolution in man.'

"He says: 'This evolution is towards a transcendental state of consciousness which has characterized the Buddha, Christ, Vyassa, Shankaracharys and all great luminaries of mankind. I am trying to show through empirical research that this condition of consciousness is the ultimate target of human evolution.' "

If the target is this higher plateau described by Gopi Krishna, the experience is apparently accompanied by a heightened sense of energy flowing within the body. A discussion of this is being incorporated here because a number of people have reported experiencing these sensations while meditating inside pyramids. This is not to say that these experiences are a prelude to the rising of the kundalini, but there are some similarities involved and if by chance that is what is happening, a greater understanding is required.

Persons who are interested in pyramids are for the most part also interested in self-growth, they are reaching toward new horizons. Because they are people on a journey, many are involved in growth activities, such as meditation, Yoga, Tai Chi, and so on. If these efforts have been of benefit to them, they are focusing their energies in ways designed to produce transcendental states. Their use of the pyramid may contribute to this goal. On the other hand, if new experiences have occurred, the pyramid may be simply a coincidental site. In any case, questions have been raised as to the nature of the phenomena and we believe it is necessary to discuss the kundalini experience. Whether or not it coincides with pyramid experience, the reader will need to determine this for himself. It is our belief, however, that a correspondence does exist which we will relate shortly.

A description of the nature of kundalini energy and its relationship to heightened states of awareness and functioning must be prefaced by a brief discussion of human psychophysiological systems as understood in Yoga, the school that has thus far provided us most of the information on kundalini.

According to Yoga traditions, man passes through three major levels of functioning: physical, psychic, and noetic. On the physical level, life is expressed through the senses; on the psychic level, through a bioelectrical dimension known as the centers or chakras; and when life's currents reach the noetic plateau of expression, energy is balanced in the completely activated centers and flows along a middle channel, putting the awakened individual in tune with universal forces.

The Yoga system conceives that in the average man the senses, organs, and so forth are activated by the vital energy being monitored and directed by the endocrine glands: adrenals, thyroid, pituitary, and so on. When sufficient development has been realized at the physical level, man is ready for the next evolutionary step, the psychic.

With this second crossing (the first being the development of the outer brain and self-consciousness), the physical body and its endocrine system activate new energy centers, the chakras. Vital energy, prana, then flows through both the physical body and the psychic envelope with its seven additional centers of response.

The Tibetan concept of how universal energy or consciousness evolves throughout nature should help illustrate how these forces work to carry man through a series of steps leading to samadhi or enlightenment. According to this model, mineral substances are constructed of dense physical matter with a slight expansion of etheric matter; plants consist of physical, etheric, and a slight expansion of emotional matter (one is reminded of Backster's experiments in recording the emotional response of plants); animals consist of physical, etheric, emotional, and a slight expansion of mental matter; and the human is constructed of physical, etheric, emotional, mental, and a slight expansion of spiritual matter at this point in his development.

Within Yoga psychophysiological concepts, man is composed of seven bodies, one transposed upon the other in this order: physical; etheric; astral or emotional or desire body; lower manas or lower mental, sometimes viewed as the rational mind; higher manas, or intuitive mind; soul; and atman or pure spirit. Integrated within the visible and invisible components of man and creating the bridge from man's physical to his spiritual nature are the seven chakras mentioned above. These are located within the etheric and higher bodies rather than in the physical. This is the dimension of the body now under investigation by Western bioelectrical medicine. The chakras are not visible to ordinary sight but can be seen by clairvoyants and resemble round, spinning wheels from which the word "chakra" is derived. The chakras are located in the vicinity of their endocrine counterparts, and as the endocrine system controls in large part the activities of the physical body, so the chakras determine the activities of the psychic body. The chakras are located in the vicinity of the base of the spine, reproductive organs, solar plexus, heart, throat, pituitary, and pineal.

In psychic awakening, energy is activated in the chakras and man becomes aware of himself and his world in different ways than before the awakening. He is conscious of dimensions of life which were beyond the range of his physical senses to detect. Rather than just effects, he becomes more aware of causes; rather than seeing only "things," he becomes sensitive to energy fields, and cognizant of the oneness of life. Although he may find it difficult to describe, he will allude to higher states of consciousness; and he will likely develop some paranormal powers. The latter should not be confused, however, with lower levels of psychic experiences which man shares in common with other animals, sometimes referred to as negative psychism and a product of the inner brain.

There is some evidence to support the belief that a growing number of persons are experiencing this level of awakening. It is also believed that legitimate efforts to gain elevated states of consciousness through meditation, biofeedback, and so on and exercises to develop psychic sensitivity will quicken this experience. With a growing number of persons using pyramids in which to meditate—and many of these practitioners reporting heightened levels of awareness and sensitivity, including visual and feeling — we are forced to ask ourselves what influence the pyramid may have on these experiences.

"Six weeks ago I constructed a six-foot tall pyramid in a spare room. I have been using it to meditate in twice a day. Shortly after initiating this schedule, I began seeing auras around people. I thought that it might be my imagination but then I had the opportunity to check what I was seeing against that of an individual who has read auras for many years. My version was nearly identical to hers . . ." This note from a graduate student in social work at the University of Kansas is representative of the many letters we have received on this subject.

As mentioned earlier, the pyramid may contribute little to such experiences. It may be coincidence or sitting in the pyramid may stimulate a certain frame of mind. Still, it is difficult to ignore the fact that so many reports state that these experiences did not precede the use of pyramids. And when we think of everything being some form of energy, it is not difficult to envision that unusual or enhanced forces inside the pyramid could have an effect on the energy flow within the human body.

The chakras, or energy vortices, are activated by means of energy flowing up two channels along the spine. Yoga refers to these as the Ida (negative) and Pingala (positive) currents. If the energy flow through these channels is not balanced, problems can develop—including mental aberrations, disease, perversion of drives, talents, skills, and so forth—and in its milder form of erratic movement, unwar-

Seven chakras or centers of energy in man according to Yoga

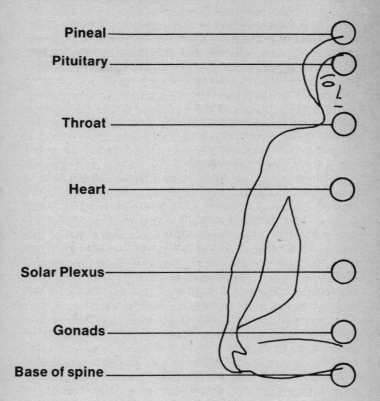

Pineal

Pituitary

Throat

Heart

Solar Plexus

Gonads

Base of spine

ranted fatigue may occur. The irregular flow can be caused by misdirected repressions, negative thoughts and actions, alcohol and drug addiction, the wrong diets for this level of development, ill-advised techniques for developing psychic talents, and complex breathing exercises for which the person is not prepared. This subject is explored further in several chapters but we might note here that on occasion people tell us they have experienced unpleasant feelings while inside pyramids. If the force field within the pyramid is activating the individual's energy flow, discomfort would be felt if the system is not balanced. One case comes to mind that would tend to confirm this. A high school senior, the son of neighbors, became interested in Yoga and shortly thereafter constructed a meditation-size pyramid. A week after he started using it, he paid me a visit. He said he wanted to pursue meditation inside his pyramid but every time he tried he became so tense that meditation was impossible. After some discussion, it was learned that he was putting his body through some very stress-producing hatha Yoga postures for which he had not prepared himself, and further, he was trying some complicated breathing exercises that he had found in a book and for which he was equally unprepared. He was advised to rest for a week from any posture or breathing exercises and then resume them with very simple ones and not to overdo them. A month later he told me he was feeling much more relaxed inside his pyramid and better able to meditate inside than outside. Another young aspirant to transcendental states went on an extremely harsh diet without the benefit of medical advice and experienced headaches and nausea while inside a pyramid. Her system was unable to handle the intensified field, it would seem, but wiser eating habits produced the desired results without physical discomfort.

Once the psychic awakening has occurred the way is prepared for the third crossing. Of this occurrence, Gopi Krishna states in *The Awakening of the Kundalini*, ". . . The power behind the extraordinary performances of spiritual geniuses and the force behind psychic phenomena are both the outflow of a springhead of intelligent energy, present in the human organism . . . The vital energy of the body converges toward this transformation."

And in *Higher Consciousness* Krishna explains:

"Those who attained to the state of transhuman consciousness invariably demonstrated irrefutable evidence of lofty traits of character and conduct. The life stories of all well-known mystics, seers, and prophets are testimony to this fact. This is the target of the evolutionary process for us all, and the entire human race is evolving toward the state of what we associate with the heavenly and the divine. There have been, and can be, no concessions and special privileges in a system of creation rooted in law. We are all part of one evolutionary process."

According to our model, the heightened activity in the chakras, culminating in the intense vitalization of the pituitary, draws the "divine" spark from the universal energy, and it attracts the sleeping energy at the base of the spine. Like a blinding light, a burst of radiant energy, or the awareness of a great fire within, described by Dr. Bucke, the kundalini flashes through the body, spinning the chakras at great speed and illuminating the mind. It is called the serpent's fire in some literature because mystics have described the energy as a great serpent coiled two and a half times and sleeping at the base of the spine or "mulahara" chakra. When activated, it strikes quickly and with great force. It is believed to be this power radiating in the seventh center, or pineal, that was depicted by Renaissance painters as the halo around the head of holy persons.

Referring to a painting by the well-known Armenian artist Mihran K. Serailian, Manly Palmer Hall, in a short essay on the opening of the third eye, stated, "This painting of the head of Minerva shows, in part, the activities of the pineal gland and the pituitary body at the time of the phenomenon commonly termed 'the opening of the Third Eye.' The kundalini fire is seen rising upward through the spinal column into the pons of the medulla oblongata. The golden light radiating from the base of the brain, at the back, gradually increases in size and intensity until it forms the nimbus, or halo, of the saint. The pituitary body is here shown surrounded by an elliptic rose aura. The pineal gland—the Third Eye of the Mysteries—is here depicted as blue in color and surrounded by a radiating blue aura. In reality, however, this aura includes within itself all the colors of the spectrum, but blue decidedly predominates. The tiny vibrating finger on the pineal gland points directly toward the pituitary body. This finger, vibrating at a very high rate of speed, is the actual cause of true spiritual illumination."

When the kundalini rises, it follows the "straight and narrow way," the center channel lying between the Ida and Pingala. In Yoga this is referred to as the Sushumna. According to informed authorities but contrary to some recent popular writing on the subject, during psychic awakening only the five inner centers, lying between the base of the spine and the pineal, are activated. This awakening was known to the Egyptian Mystery Schools as the Lunar Cycle. The third crossing, the noetic awakening, was known as the Solar Cycle or the Passage of the Sun God. With noetic awakening, all seven centers are vivified.

In one of the lessons given to his students, Vitvan, a profound teacher of some twenty-five years ago, stated, "Much confusion will be saved if the student in the teleotic work understands that the release of the Ida-Pingala currents and the awakening of those currents in the centers symbolized by the 'Journey' is the purificatory period on the Path of Attainment . . . Then after the completion of the 'Journey of the Moon,' symbolically speaking, follows what the Greeks called the good aspect to the function of the force in all centers, in that phase representing the culmination of the Individualizing Process—symbolized as the 'Sun's Journey.' "

As far as can be learned, the concepts of the seven centers in man were taught simultaneously in India and Egypt. In order to trace the earliest divisions of the Zodiacal wheel and establish its significance in the symbolical portrayal of the awakening of the centers or to what some of the literature refers to as the "Opening of the Seals," one must direct his attention, it would seem, to the ancient

Egyptians. This is important to us in our study, for it throws some light on what the Egyptians knew and would therefore have likely incorporated into the Great Pyramid, their greatest-known structure.

Even the shape of the pyramid seems to represent the sevenfold nature of man. The square base can be seen as the four lower principles of man, his physical, etheric, astral, and lower manas or mind. These are the divisions which, according to the teachings, are mortal and disintegrate upon death. They are of the earth and the base of the pyramid rests solidly upon it. The triangular sides can be seen as the trinity, man's three higher principles, higher manas or mind, soul, and spirit, which are immortal and leave the body upon death. Symbolical of man's being and destiny, he builds the base first—must experience and conquer the earthly kingdom first—then constructs the sides—develops his spiritual nature—and finally reaches the apex—his nature converges toward the unity and oneness of God, for here the pyramid is no longer divided but is a single point. It is interesting to note that the only projection of a square to a single point forms a pyramid, just as the only transcendence of man's fourfold lower nature to the oneness of God is by way of the triangle, the three higher principles.

Several persons have told us that while meditating inside pyramids they have suddenly experienced mental visions of squares, triangles, and circles. Sometimes they flow in and out, create patterns, fade, and come back again more intense than ever. One person said that geometrical figures danced before him and he could still see them after he opened his eyes.

Probably one of the earlier symbols used by the Egyptians was the divided circle. It is believed that the circle was used to symbolize the whole cosmic process as well as a complete cycle or smaller circle therein. This likely was the cycle of each human being.

"In carrying out their symbolism of the Wisdom," Vitvan states in his lessons, "the Egyptians divided their country in half—upper and lower Egypt or the North Half and the South Half. Today in our understanding and instruction, the total activity of the Mother Substance is labeled the Cosmic Process. This division of the circle in half by the Egyptians had an application relative to each turn in the spiraling process, or to each sphere (represented by each turn) in the multiplicity of spheres representing the totality of the Mother (the Egyptian goddess Isis).

"Of the many applications made by the Egyptians of the divided circle, we are chiefly concerned with one—namely, that applied to the individual as a whole or the Individualizing Process. The South Half of the circle represented the focalization of consciousness in the psychic-nature. (The entire Lunar Cycle represents the period to lift or direct the focus of consciousness with accompanying forces out or above the psychic-nature.) The upper or North Half of the circle represented the focalization of consciousness in the Mind-level. The dividing line between was called 'the Horizon,' and the final battle (the real Armageddon) is always fought out on this line.

"The term 'Pharaoh' in Egyptian symbology represented the Sun God (the individualized aspect of Self). What mystified Egyptologists (in studying tablets of stone, etc.) was why, when a new Pharaoh was seated or enthroned his first act was to marshal all of his armies, proceed with them to the dividing line between the North and South Half of his country, and stage a simulated war to reconquer the South Half. This merely graphically portrayed the necessity for 'the Conqueror' (the seated Sun God) to retain supremacy of the psychic-nature. As the Pharaoh had to literally bring all of his kingdom under complete control, so, symbolically the conquering individualized Self must maintain constant control over his own 'South Half' . . . i.e., the psychic-nature.

"Another point which mystified the Egyptologists is that in the story of Horus and Osiris the part of Osiris for which Horus sought were buried in 'lower Egypt' but when Horus found them, one after another he took them North to put them together; and lo and behold Osiris became whole and alive again.

"As the parts of each soul and every one of us are buried in the Darkness of our respective psychic-natures (mummy wrappings), so each shall be resurrected in the 'North Half' or Mind-level of his Individualized Sphere."

Manly Palmer Hall, president of the Philosophical Research Society, Los Angeles, and internationally recognized authority on the ancient mystery schools, states in *The Secret Teachings of All Ages:*

"Through the mystic passageways and chambers of the Great Pyramid passed the illumined of antiquity. They entered its portals as men; they came forth as gods. It was the place of the 'second birth,' the 'womb of the Mysteries,' and wisdom dwelt in it as God dwells in the hearts of men . . . The modern knows little of these ancient rites. The scientist and the theologian alike gaze upon the sacred structure, wondering what fundamental urge inspired the herculean labor. If they would but think for a moment, they would realize that there is only one urge in the soul of man capable of supplying the required incentive—namely, the desire to know, to understand, and to exchange the narrowness of human mortality for the greater breadth and scope of living enlightenment. So men say of the Great Pyramid that it is the most perfect building in the world, the source of weights and measures, the original Noah's Ark, the origin of languages, alphabets, and scale of temperature and humidity. Few realize, however, that it is the gateway to the Eternal."

If, as it seems, the ancient Egyptians were aware of the various dimensions of man and their teachings were designed to "open the seals," was this knowledge in some fashion contained within the Great Pyramid? If it was the site of the secret initiations, was it also an instrument of initiation? Is there something about its structure that lends itself to activating the energy fields within man?

These questions cannot be answered directly, of course, because the reason for its construction has been lost in the dim recesses of prehistory. Beyond what we can learn of the ancient mystery schools, we have only the Great Pyramid itself with which to work . . . and now replicas modeled after it.

In the Eastern tradition it is believed that an advanced human being, one who has experienced spiritual awakening, can transfer some of this energy to another person in such a manner as to elevate his consciousness. Is the pyramid our guru, teaching us to look within ourselves for answers and energizing us in a way to awaken our spiritual nature? There is an old saying that when the chela (student) is ready, his guru will appear. Are we launched into pyramid research at this time because we are ready for a new evolutionary step?

"I know this sounds strange but when I am inside my pyramid I feel as though I am in the presence of an elevated being." The speaker was a young engineer who told us that he had been religious all of his life and had felt since childhood a certain reverence for life. He said that once before in his life he had experienced this feeling of being in the presence of a great force. This was when he was about twelve and met a famous missionary.

Whatever the reason, whatever the cause, people are experiencing new sensitivities, new feelings and thoughts from sleeping, meditating, or just sitting for a while in pyramids.

We have an acquaintance who was a technical writer for a government bureau in Washington, D.C., for many years. She was familiar with the literature on human-growth potentialities, transcendental states, and so on, and yet she had never experienced anything close, she claimed, to altered states of consciousness, psychic awareness, intuition, or creative insights. She said she couldn't even recall her dreams. Deciding to do something about it, she took six-weeks' leave of absence from her job and plunged into a "crash program for enlightenment." With the help of informed authorities involved in research into the voluntary control of internal states of awareness, she designed a program that, except for a few hours of sleep each night, would keep her involved in an intensive search for ex-

Series of 27 4-inch cardboard pyramids used beneath bed in midwestern home to promote restfulness.

panded consciousness and sensitivity. Her itinerary included biofeedback, meditation, Yoga exercises, breathing
techniques, chanting, some discussion and reading, but
strictly limited to the pursuit of the new self. It was all very
neat, well-planned, and not just a compiling of various
techniques as one might suppose. Now, one interesting
aspect of this plan was that she did much of her meditation,
breathing exercises, and reading inside a wooden pyramid.

She dove in with great enthusiasm; she emerged with
even more. For at the end of the six weeks she had experienced some very worthwhile "highs" in her meditation;
had moved from producing very little alpha and no theta
on the electroencephalograph to a great deal of low alpha
and quite a little theta, the contemplative state of seasoned
meditators; was demonstrating a considerable amount of
control over her involuntary nervous system, as monitored
by biofeedback devices; had experienced recognizable intuitive insights for the first time in her life; was recalling her
dreams and they were becoming more and more organized;
and the creative urge was so strong she was painting, writing poetry, and had started on a play. A real success story
with a happy ending.

This woman, of course, may be an exception. Obviously
she had desire, determination, a definite goal, a plan, faith,
stamina, and she was able to take six weeks out of her life
to accomplish her goal. But she did not become a legend
in her own time, for many others have realized these goals,
although perhaps not in this condensed period of time. The
point is, however, that the goals are real enough, worthwhile, and accessible. And, if we can believe our own experiences and those of others, the pyramid possibly may
present another approach to amplifying or enriching one's
efforts to expand awareness and self-knowledge.

In Dr. Karan Singh's speech at the "Yoga, Science and
Man" seminar mentioned earlier he also said, "It is now
well established that we are using a fraction of the capaci-
ties of the human brain; this has been widely accepted by
neurosurgeons and scientists. Now it is possible that the
next step in human development could be the activization

of those areas of the human brain which are at present unused or unknown."

Can the pyramid contribute to this next step? There are reasons to think so.

5

The Twilight Zone

A strange place where time is distorted, the scenes misty, appearing from nowhere, and fading again. Faces are there, vague, sometimes haunting, new ones, and forgotten ones suddenly taking on an importance they were not afforded before. The language is vague, spoken with meaning but is meaningless. There seems to be a general acceptance of the bizarre in this place, but if you ask what is going on, you are shown a picture and another and another until you forget the question. You start running . . . no, you are flying, or just floating . . . you're not sure.

You have entered the twilight zone. You've been here before. As a matter of fact most of us spend nearly one-third of our lives in this place and yet it remains as foreign to us as that night when we first crossed its borders.

"For dream is an entry into the first hinterland of the mind," Paul Brunton once stated. "The process of dreaming fascinates savage and savant alike," he said.

Easy chair inside plastic pyramid in midwestern home.

"It possesses a mystery and magic of its own. How do they originate, these strange night plays which are often performed by many actors but never witnessed by an audience of more than one?"

Dreams might be described as a condition widespread among men and the higher animals in which the pupils become extremely small, the eyelids closed or nearly so, the amount of air in the lungs falls sharply, as does the secretion of digestive juice, saliva, and urine. The heart slows way down and brainwaves shift to another wavelength. That's the physiological description but it tells us very little about how we experience them or about their contents.

Lyall Watson tells us in *Super Nature*, "Proper dreaming occurs during sleep, but it is not just a part of ordinary sleep. Orthodox sleep alternates several times during the night with periods of a very different, almost paradoxical, kind of sleep. In orthodox sleep the brain produces big, slow waves of delta rhythm, the eyes are still, and the heartbeat is regular, but some of the muscles, and particularly those of the throat, are still tense. In paradoxical sleep the brain produces more rapid waves, almost like those of wakefulness, the eyes move rapidly to and fro, and the heartbeat becomes irregular, but despite all the mental activity going on, the muscles of the body, including those of the throat, are more relaxed and the sleeper is much more difficult to awake."

The study of dreams was not taken seriously by Western science until Freud used the interpretation of dreams as an entry to the unconscious mind. Jung discovered the universal quality of dreams in archetypal symbols, and when it was learned that rapid eye movement corresponded to the dreaming state, dreams became a legitimate subject of scientific investigation because something physical could be measured. With a growing understanding of the importance of the unconscious mind as the largest part of the mental iceberg, most researchers today consider the examination of sleep and dream states imperative to understanding the functions of the mind.

These investigators have started saying, "Pay attention to your dreams," echoing an axiom long held by the mystics. Dreams are being afforded more sober reflection in an age toying with new concepts of matter and consciousness. With the new physics saying that the universe is not a collection of things but an expression of energy fields and even hinting that beyond that it appears more like consciousness than anything, the subjective realm has taken on the greater vesture of reality. Science doesn't talk any more of reality as though it was some product to be measured and weighed; it speaks of levels of realities and functional sets, meaning that reality exists as a set of conditions to something that observes it. In this ball game the dream is one of those reality sets because it is a state of unique awareness, and when physical matter was dismissed from the universe the only thing left to measure was awareness.

For a long time it was believed that dreams were only our drives, fears, hopes, repressions, frustrations, guilts, complexes, wishes, fantasies, or whatever, pushed down into the unconscious from the conscious where they struggled for understanding and expression. We were told to look at our dreams in order to understand ourselves better, including those facets of our personality that our conscious minds either refused to accept or failed to understand.

This approach is still viable and evidently continues to bear fruit and most scholars agree that our lives are largely directed by our unconscious minds. Since it cannot be examined directly it must be explored secondhand by inference. But there is a growing suspicion that dreams are not limited to sorting through the castoffs of the conscious mind. There are additional inputs to awareness from sources beyond the range of the rational mind. Further than this, greater attention is now being focused on the mystical tradition which assures us that in some aspects of the dream state our awareness shifts to other planes or levels of reality.

This is where pyramids enter the picture. We have been hearing from persons sitting, sleeping, and meditating inside pyramids who tell us that their dream experiences have increased, their sleep is different though more restful, their dreams are more vivid, organized, and have greater meaning to them.

Other pyramid investigators are saying much the same thing. Bill Kerrell and Kathy Goggin quote correspondents in *The Guide to Pyramid Energy:*

" 'It feels light and similar to sleeping in the mountains above 8,000 feet.'

" 'My dreams have become more vivid and colorful, and I'm able to remember more of them.'

" 'On awakening I can still feel the vibrations going through my body, and I feel great!'

" 'I feel fresher in the morning and more alert during the day. My dreams have become more vivid, suggesting that I'm releasing thought stresses during sleep.' "

Whether the pyramid has a direct bearing on this would, of course, be difficult to say. However, a great many of the people reporting are not aware that others are saying the same things and the consistency of the reports would seem to indicate some influencing factor. In any case, the quality of sleep and dreams has changed and this is the phenomenon that we must consider.

What is the message in the dream? In *Wisdom of the Overself* Paul Brunton states, "For if some dreams are symbolic and bear interpretation, many others are not and mean nothing more than what their surface shows; if some reveal repressed sex wishes most of the others are blamelessly innocent; and if some are reconstructed out of the materials supplied by wakeful experience others are entirely new constructions."

Later in the same chapter, "Studies in Dreams," Brunton says, "A purely materialist explanation of dreams will not account for all of them. Nor is it right to assert, as some ancient Indian and modern Western psychoanalytic schools assert, that our dreams draw their material solely from waking experience, past or present, forgotten or remembered. For the mind is not only reproductive but also productive; it can not only reproduce figures and things already known in our waking life but also produce figures and things never known in our waking life; it can not only recall accumulated impressions of the past but also foresee or even create impressions of the future . . ."

What, we must ask ourselves, does a dream such as the following one of Tom Garrett's mean? He states that he was not asleep and yet his experience has all the qualities of a dream:

"As I became increasingly relaxed I began a series of mental images. The images were dream-like but not dreams as I was fully awake. These images took the form of the Great Pyramid of Gizeh. These images were extremely realistic and I actually felt as if I were viewing the real thing. I would view the pyramid from the apex downward, then circle the structure at about mid-point range; then from the base looking upward. These images were complete with the sensation of warm sunshine and an arid quality to the air around the pyramid image.

"I perceived these images as reality, yet at the same time separated from total consciousness. With later reflection it occurred to me that the images had appeared dream-like—somewhat like being able to view a dream in the sub-conscious mind while in a relaxed, waking state. I was surprised later to remember how casually I accepted the pyramid images while they were occurring and how astounded I was when I thought about it later.

"That night my wife, Mary, who had also sat in the pyramid that day, and myself had dreams identical in nature. Our sleep was broken and we were both dreaming of triangular and pyramidal shapes that seemed to be approaching us at very high speeds, then breaking away or just going through us."

This sharing of a dream brings us an interesting facet of the dream experience. Recent research of Drs.

Montague Ullman and Stanley Krippner at the Dream Laboratory of the Maimonides Medical Center in New York City indicates that mental telepathy functions better during the dream rather than the waking state and is not an uncommon experience. Psychologist Dr. Gertrude Schmeidler, in commenting on their work, stated, "The clear conclusion to be drawn . . . is that dream reports can show the effect of telepathy, clairvoyance, and precognition . . . a striking conclusion, worthy of a massive effort."

The dean of American parapsychologists, Dr. Garner Murphy, states in the Foreword of the book written by Ullman, Krippner and Alan Vaughan, *Dream Telepathy*, "Dreams can carry a message through channels other than the channels of the senses. This has long been suspected. Indeed, it has been the subject of both theory and practice from the ancient civilizations of China and Egypt to the period of modern parapsychology."

Working with the hypothesis that ESP is more commonly found in the dreaming state than the waking state, the team conducted experiments for ten years to determine if a person acting as an "agent" could send his thoughts to the mind of a sleeping subject, thereby influencing the subject's dreams. Their results clearly prove their hypothesis and also reveal that glimpses into the future do occur in the dream state.

It would seem that the mind in the dream state is not bounded by space or time limitations. The dreamer can apparently go back or forward in time and can travel through space, occasionally viewing a scene many miles distant and providing an accurate description even though never having been there while awake.

In order to deal with this phenomenon in any sort of satisfactory fashion we need a model somewhat expanded from the one utilizing only the unconscious mind. This is too simplistic and fails to take into consideration paranormal powers demonstrated during the dream state and the reporting of information not to be found in the conscious and unconscious minds.

We get some clue as to what transpires during sleep from the following Edgar Cayce reading:

". . . There is an active force within each individual that functions in the manner of a sense when the body-physical is in sleep, repose or rest . . . this we have chosen to call a sixth sense . . . this sixth sense is the activating power or force of the other self . . . when the physical consciousness is at rest, the other self communes with the soul of the body, see? Or it goes out into that realm of . . . all experiences of that entity . . . throughout the eons of time . . . What, then, is the sixth sense? Not the soul, not the conscious mind, not the subconscious mind, not intuition alone, not any of these cosmic forces—but the very force or activity of the soul in its experience of that soul itself." (No. 754-2.)

Keeping in mind our earlier description of the seven principles or envelopes of the human body, it is the contention of this tradition that consciousness can be contained by other envelopes or bodies than the physical one. The etheric body, however, is actually a less dense aspect of the physical body, and its consciousness, therefore, is merely an expression of consciousness derived from its physical counterpart. It is believed that in order to dream consciousness must shift from the physical to the etheric. But inasmuch as the etheric is merely an auric or electrical projection of the physical, the content of the dream is merely an outpouring of subconscious fragments.

While most of our dreams will be of the above nature, there are other dreams which take on different and unique qualities. These dreams seem to be of a substance that gives them a greater reality. They are clearer, more organized, usually educational, and more easily recalled, sometimes even years later. We may find it difficult at the time that they occur to describe how they are different, but we are quite sure they are. In these dreams we may have contact with persons who have passed on; we may experience other persons whom we may meet physically for the first time months or years later. We may travel to distant places and collect information that upon checking proves to be accurate.

According to our model, when such dreams occur, consciousness has shifted from the etheric to the next level, the astral, and this envelope can serve as a vehicle of consciousness. The astral is another plane of reality with its own set of experiences and its own occupants, including persons such as ourselves on mentally projected trips but also including those who no longer possess a physical body as we experience one. We can meet, according to this model, on the astral plane as it can serve as a common base between physically oriented beings and those on higher planes of existence.

Out-of-the-body experiences are now being investigated in dream laboratories, two of the principal ones being at Maimonides and at the University of California at Davis under the direction of psychologist Dr. Charles Tart. The subjects are monitored during sleep by a number of psycho-physiological measurements, including brainwaves. If a subject demonstrates an ability to project mentally and report accurately from this vantage point, he is given a particular assignment. He is told that when he finds himself separate from his physical body he is to go to a particular place and read a message placed there by the researchers. The findings reveal that a number of subjects have been able to do this. Out-of-the-body experiences have become so common that they are simply referred to by investigators by the initials "OBE."

Several years ago while attending the Interdisciplinary Conference on Voluntary Control of Internal States, sponsored by the Menninger Foundation, we had the opportunity to spend some time with Bob Monroe, author of the book *Journeys Out of the Body*. Monroe, a Charlottesville, Virginia, businessman, was there to participate in the program and report on some nine hundred logged trips he had allegedly taken outside his body. At that time his experiences had been investigated by several laboratories and he has devoted a considerable amount of his time to research since that particular conference, partly due to the interest he generated in the ninety scientists from several countries who were in attendance.

Monroe related to several of us during a coffee break that after he had gained some acquaintance with the nature of the astral plane, his life there had become as organized and consistent as his life on the physical plane and that he actually attended school on that level. He described to us his traveling experiences and stated that his main concern was obtaining data that could be verified on this level by disinterested observers. Apparently he was somewhat successful in this pursuit.

When I think of our own experiences and those of others with vivid dreams while sleeping inside the pyramid, I remember the conversations with Monroe. I am amazed at the number of seemingly parallel experiences, even though, perhaps, Monroe is a much more seasoned traveler and therefore a more perceptive reporter.

Discussing the nature of the dream experience as it relates to the level we have been referring to as the astral plane (which he refers to as the "desire body"), Max Heindel stated in *The Rosicrucian Cosmo-Conception*, a book published in 1911 but still widely read today:

"At first their motion is slow and hard to bring about, but by degrees the sense-centers of the desire body will make places for themselves within the dense and vital bodies, which learn to accommodate themselves to this new activity. Then some day, when the proper life has developed the requisite cleavage between the higher and lower parts of the vital body, there is a supreme effort of the will; a spiral motion in many directions takes place, and the aspirant stands outside his dense body. He looks at it as at another person. The door of his prison-house has been opened. He is free to come and go, as much at liberty in the inner worlds as in the physical world, functioning at will, in the inner or outer world, a helper of all desiring his services in any of them.

"Before the aspirant learns to voluntarily leave the

body, he may have worked in the desire body during sleep, for in some people the desire body becomes organized before the separation can be brought about in the vital body. Under those conditions it is impossible to bring back these subjective experiences to waking consciousness, but generally in such cases it will be noticed, as the first sign of development, that all confused dreams will cease. Then, after a while, the dreams will become more vivid and perfectly logical. The aspirant will dream of being in places and with people (whether known to him in waking hours or not matters little), conducting himself in as reasonable a way as if he were in the waking state. If the place of which he dreams is accessible to him in waking hours, he may sometimes get proof of the reality of his dream if he will note some physical detail of the scene and verify his nocturnal impression next day."

There is an interesting footnote regarding Heindel, who has been dead many years. We have a friend who has had experiences similar to those of Bob Monroe. One day he was relating some of these to several of us and told us that on the other plane he was being instructed by "a very profound teacher. His name is Max something or the other . . ." He described him and told us about some of the lessons. After a minute the member of the group in whose house we were gathered left the room and came back with a picture. "Could this be your instructor?" he asked. Our friend was speechless for a moment and finally sputtered, "That's him . . . that's him! Who . . . how did you get his picture?"

"Well," the second friend replied, "this is a picture of Max Heindel. He was a highly regarded teacher and writer for many years a half century ago . . ."

"He's still highly regarded," our traveling friend answered, "but I had never heard of him before on this plane."

"And he still looks like this?" one of us asked.

"Yes, but, you see, if he was well known on this plane, there are those there who still see him, I imagine, as they knew him on earth . . . so he likely retains this image for that reason."

The technical writer mentioned earlier, who underwent an intensive program day and night for six weeks in order to experience transcendental states, finally realized a creative flow for the first time in her life. This is also apparently happening to people spending some time inside pyramids. They are apparently moving into theta brainwaves, stilling cortical activities in favor of the intuitive, or experiencing some breakthrough in psychic awakening through activating the chakras, depending on which model we choose to use. Another model that fits in with the above has to do with shifting into the twilight zone between waking and sleeping. This is the place where there seems to occur an input to the awareness that cannot be traced to the conscious or unconscious minds. This outside source is sometimes referred to as the superconscious or is what Emerson called the "Oversoul" or Brunton the "Overself." The images that flood the awareness in this state are referred to by scientists as "hypnagogic imagery."

In a paper, "Voluntary Control of Internal States: Psychological and Physiological," written by Dr. Elmer Green, Alyce Green, and Dale Walters, and presented at the 1969 International Congress of Cybernetics, it was stated, "The 'reverie' which accompanies the semiconscious production of theta waves and low-frequency alpha seems to be associated with and make possible, under certain conditions, the detection of hypnagogic-like imagery, the sine qua non of creativity for many outstanding people . . ."

Aldous Huxley mentioned several times in his writing that his best ideas came to him while he was in a state of reverie. Robert Louis Stevenson stated that the plots for his stories were given to him in dreams by the "brownies" in his mind. Einstein claimed that he did not reason out the theory of relativity but that it came to him. Friedrich Kekulé urged his contemporaries in science, "Let us learn to dream, gentlemen," after a series of dreams led to his famous discovery, which has been called "the most brilliant piece of prediction to be found in the whole range of organic chemistry." Through the dreamed symbol of a snake biting its tail, Kekulé derived the revolutionary proposal that some organic compounds occur in closed chains or rings.

"When physicist Niels Bohr was a student, he had a vivid dream in which he was on a sun composed of burning gas. Planets whistled by him as they revolved around the sun, to which they were attached by thin filaments. Suddenly, the gas sun cooled and solidified, the planets crumbled away. When Bohr awoke he realized that he had conceived the model of the atom. The sun was the fixed center around which electrons revolved, held in place by energy fields or 'quanta.' Thus," Ullman, Krippner, and Vaughan relate in *Dream Telepathy,* "in a dream was born the foundation for modern atomic physics."

The same authors also state, "The dream state is a natural arena in which creative energies are at play. Dreams tend to arrange information in unique and emotionally related ways. They break with reality-oriented thought to group things together by 'illogical' association and as a consequence new relationships emerge which can sometimes provide the breakthrough for a waiting and observant mind."

It is mystery, it is magic, but the dream is important, and it may lead us to greater realities than we have known. If sitting in pyramids means also to poise on the threshold of new knowledge, it might be well for us to paraphrase Kekulé with the admonition, "Let us learn to dream in the pyramid, gentlemen."

6

A Breath of Fresh Air

Smoke filled the crowded restaurant, saturating the air with a gray, unpleasant aura. We glanced about the room but the only table available was located in the midst of this hovering residue.

"Would you prefer to go elsewhere?" Normally we would have given little thought to the client's atmospheric contribution. Yet we were aware of it on this occasion and felt apologetic because our dinner guest was a yogi highly regarded for his ability to demonstrate considerable control over psychophysiological states. Each day he spent several hours doing breathing exercises and meditation in preparing his body for the strenuous demands made upon it. We thought the cigarette and cigar smoke might be offensive to him.

"No, this place is fine," he said. "It doesn't matter." As we sat down, he added, "We will create our own atmosphere." A provocative statement, but before we could ask for an explanation he proceeded to demonstrate.

He took his napkin from the table, folded it several times, and for a moment held it between his two hands. Then he shook it slowly three times above the table. If a door or window had suddenly been thrown open, filling the room with fresh air, it would not have been more effective. The smoke in our vicinity of the restaurant disappeared. It did not return during our sojourn.

Silently the yogi handed us the napkin and motioned that we should smell it. It was permeated with a pleasant scent of lemon.

". . . The air inside is unmistakably different. It is fresher and have you noticed that there is a faint scent of lemon?"

She had been inside the pyramid for less than an hour, not really trying to meditate but allowing her thoughts to drift. It was pleasant, she said, not to feel compelled to do anything but simply "to be." A compulsive worker, she usually felt uncomfortable "not doing something constructive. Even when I sit down for a few minutes, I end up problem-solving."

But this was "another world" and she became acutely aware of the fresh air and the scent of lemon after daydreaming with her eyes closed and seeing herself walking through a flower garden alone. She opened her eyes, the garden disappeared, but not the fresh air and the lemon scent.

We both had noticed the fresh air inside the pyramids shortly after starting our research but did not discover the other's awareness of this until sharing notes one evening. We laughed about it, noted that it probably had some significance, but it went into the file as an interesting observation and was more or less forgotten until others started reporting the same experience.

". . . While smoking a cigarette in the pyramid I noticed that the smoke seemed to disappear rather than settle in the structure. I tried for several minutes to discover where the smoke was going, but it only seemed to just 'go away,' " Tom Garrett told us, and added, "This has been noticed by several of my friends and seems to be one of the most interesting items due to the fact that it doesn't make sense if you use your normal frame of reference to try to explain it."

If we think in terms of the space inside the pyramid as being filled merely with air, there would seem to be little reason for the air being fresher inside an enclosure than outside; actually, one would expect the opposite. On the other hand, if we expand our frame of reference regarding space and think of it as containing a vast range of possible energy fields, we can enlarge our field of inquiry.

In Yoga breathing exercises the student is instructed in the manipulation of "prana," a word discussed elsewhere in this book and in *The Secret Power of Pyramids*. Prana means universal energy, the substance of all things, whether physical, mental, or spiritual. In addition to taking in oxygen when we breathe we also take in prana, the creator and supporter of vitality. It circulates through the nerves and through the blood vessels.

Swami Vivekananda stated, "Prana is the name for the energy that is in the universe. Whatever you see in the universe, whatever moves or works or has life is a manifestation of this prana. The sum total of the energy displayed in the universe is called prana. Before a cycle begins, prana manifests itself; it is that which is manifested as motion, as the nervous motion in human beings or animals, and the same prana is manifesting as thought, and so on . . ."

We might also refer to prana as the omnipotent force that moves the universe. Medical doctor Steven Brena, however, explains prana in Western terminology in *Yoga and Medicine:*

"What do we breathe? If I open a textbook of physiology, I find that man breathes atmospheric air, which is made up of about 20 percent oxygen and 70 percent nitrogen, the rest being various other gases. These figures are correct, but they are not all. In the air we breathe there are, besides oxygen, nitrogen, and helium, lights, sounds, colors, ultra-violet and ultra-red rays, ultra-sounds, Alpha, Beta, Gamma rays, and so on. In the atmosphere, there is an infinite variety of electromagnetic vibrations operating at different wave lengths. Some of these, very few, affect our sense organs, whereas the majority are lost to us unless we resort to special devices, such as radio, television, radar, and the like."

Brena further states, "The electromagnetic waves pierce the atmosphere, but they do not belong to the atmosphere. They are manifestations of a single energy— cosmic energy, the Hindus' Prana, that still somewhat mysterious entity which the Cosmos is made of, which in modern physics represents the only concept of its Absolute. For, in our world of relativity, the speed of light, vibratory manifestation of the Cosmos, is the only Absolute datum beyond which the human mind cannot go . . ."

But why is the air inside a pyramid as clear, as fresh as that air in the space purified by the wave of a yogi's hand? What has he done? What does a pyramid do? For several years, first with a Western teacher and later with an Eastern one, we studied the Oriental practice of pranayama, meaning the control of prana. These were breathing exercises but one soon learned that there was a great deal more going on than the mere control of one's breathing. Pranayama is believed to be the bridge between the physical and spiritual worlds. With its control, one has taken a big step toward the control of oneself and one's environment. We have seen highly trained yogis harmlessly ingest substances into their systems which would be fatal to less controlled individuals.

According to the principles of pranayama, there are actually three major levels at which one deals with his environment, including the food he ingests. With the unevolved person, living and identifying himself with physical matter, there need be little concern about noise, color, food, liquids, and so on as long as they are not poisonous or in some manner deteriorated. The person who has become aware of and sensitive to higher planes of existence, and is making an effort to grow mentally, psychically, and spiritually, finds himself being influenced by factors that previously did not affect him. Sounds soothe or distract him, and he discovers his taste in colors has changed, as may the company he keeps. Where before he could eat or drink anything, now certain foods are distasteful and may weigh him down. At this time he may become a vegetarian because meat depresses him. He is a man on a different journey requiring different fuel. The third level is that of one who has mastered control of his environment. He can meditate in Times Square, breathe deeply in a coal mine, and even eat poison itself—as we have seen them literally do—with no ill effect.

Baba Ram Das tells the story of going to India in search of the philosopher's stone. In case the trip didn't pan out too well, however, he took along a sackful of LSD tabs so he could work out his own travelogue. After some time he was placed under the keeping of a highly trained yogi and one day his guru told Baba Ram Das to bring him the sackful of acid. Although amazed that the Indian knew about the pills, he did not deny that he had them, however, and did as he was told. His teacher motioned for him to place the acid in his hand. Ram Das took one—the usual dosage for an acid trip—and placed it in his teacher's hand. The Indian still waited and several more were placed in his hand and he then swallowed them all in one fell swoop.

Ram Das was sure that he was responsible for burning out all of the little old man's circuits. Time passed and every now and then his guru would smile at him but continued with his daily exercises. Finally, Ram Das said he realized that nothing had changed within the Indian nor would it if he ate the whole sackful. He got the message. The acid was thrown away. It would no longer be needed.

Could it be that the pyramid was designed as an instrument to somehow manipulate prana in a way beneficial to man? Have a sufficient number of people become aware of the need to cleanse the body in preparation for a higher journey that this secret of the pyramid is now being made available to us? In the same manner that biofeedback equipment materialized to assist us with meditation, is the pyramid offering us the opportunity for building the bridge between body and spirit?

". . . After a period of 15 or 20 minutes I felt ready to get out of the pyramid, and upon leaving it through the door I noticed odors and realized that while in the pyramid I noticed none. Having smoked for many years, my sense of smell and taste has decreased considerably. Yet after sitting in the pyramid I was very aware of different odors."

A new sensitivity, a new awareness?

The practice of pranayama soon restores the sense of smell and taste if it has been lost as a result of our own abuses. Its continued practice brings a heightening of the senses to levels never experienced before. With this gift also comes great responsibility. The student is warned not to use his new-found awareness for sensual delights but rather as a bridge to higher consciousness. And, since he is more acutely attuned to his environment, he has to be more careful of his food, surroundings, company, etc. Odors, for example, to which he was oblivious before may now overwhelm him.

". . . That afternoon we went for Chinese food and my sense of taste was so acute that I could barely finish my meal."

There are many pranayama breathing exercises. A large number of these are not to be attempted, however, without proper training and conditioning. Where the rewards are great so are the dangers. This is not to frighten the reader for there are breathing exercises which are quite safe, but there are also those which, in controlling the flow of oxygen to the brain and the flow of bioelectrical forces, can be injurious if not practiced properly.

Since we have brought the matter up, a safe breathing exercise is as follows: sit in a relaxed position, with the back straight, and breathe in to the count of five; hold the breath momentarily and then exhale slowly to the count of ten. With eyes closed keep the attention focused entirely on the breathing. After a time you will have the feeling that "you are being breathed." This exercise should not be continued longer than five minutes in the beginning and eventually lengthened to twenty minutes. You should be entirely comfortable and relaxed while doing this exercise; if not, you are not doing it correctly. Always breathe through both nostrils; any other approach, such as alternate nostril breathing, should not be undertaken without a qualified teacher.

The above exercise will serve you well if done properly and faithfully. The Tibetans say that "the breath is the horse and mind is the rider." Breathing exercises slow down the number of breaths and to Paul Brunton in *The Search Path,* "To diminish the cycle of breaths is to curtail the supply of blood to the brain, and therefore to retard the cycle of thoughts . . . Thus the tension and relaxation of the brain, the uprising and disappearance of thoughts, correspond in peculiar harmony with the cycle of breathing and can be brought under control."

Hereward Carrington speaks of the correspondence between the breath and brainwaves in *Yoga Philosophy:*

"Here is an interesting physiological fact—If you put your hand on the wrist, you can feel the pulsation—or in the upper arm, or in the ankle or wherever there is a pulse. It simply shows the rate of the heart-beat. The pulse varies from seventy to eighty to the minute, or more, according to the degree of excitement, exercise, and so forth. That pulse-rate is the same all over the body—into the neck, the head, even the coverings of the brain. But the circulation of the brain itself is synchronous with—or correspondent to—not the heart pulsation but to the breathing rate—that is twelve to fourteen to the minute! This is a very striking fact. And it seems to show us that there is—in the circulation of the brain itself—a pulsation which is synchronous with, or correspondent to, the breathing-rate."

Carrington was writing more that fifty years ago and his

findings have since been confirmed by biofeedback techniques that, indeed, brainwaves can be slowed down and more contemplative levels reached by means of exercising breathing control.

". . . Sitting in my pyramid, I became more relaxed. My breathing, seemingly without any effort on my part, became slower and slower and thought itself seemed to disappear."

And Brunton states, "The effect upon the student of consciously dropping the rhythm of his breathing will be a pleasant relaxed mood, a calming of the constant vibration of thought, a pouring of oil upon the troubled sea of life, and a more abstracted mental condition . . ."

Breathing exercises are now being used in a number of mental hospitals as a therapeutic tool. It has been found that getting the patient to relax by means of slow, deep breathing has a tranquilizing effect. Pyramid space apparently produces a similar state of relaxation and quietude. A woman recently called and excitedly told us that her hyperactive child had settled down considerably after being inside a pyramid several times. We do not know whether this child was clinically diagnosed as hyperactive. This was the mother's term and we would not wish to give the impression that pyramids are an answer to hyperactivity. Nevertheless, we have received a sufficient number of reports on this kind of phenomena for us to believe that the pyramids do have some quieting influence.

As regards the scent of lemon in the pyramid, it has long been known that certain perfumes, such as musk oil for example, and incense can be used to establish vibratory fields of a nature to produce a certain desired effect. These effects include health, tranquillity and transcendental states.

In *The Etheric Double* A. E. Powell states, "Incense is said to act on the etheric somewhat as colours do on the astral body, and so may be employed to bring a man's vehicles rapidly into harmony. It appears that certain odours may be used to act on various parts of the brain."

Later in the book, Powell says, "An interesting set of natural talismans are those objects which produce strong scents. The gums of which incense is made, for example, can be chosen so as to be favourable to spiritual and devout thought . . ."

Scents, colors, tastes, and sounds have varying vibratory rates and a particular color will correspond to a certain sound, scent, and taste, for example. Lemon is a cleanser and purifier and the lemon scent detected in pyramids may be indicative of purifying forces at work.

In his log on pyramid experiences, Tom Garrett relates how his pyramid seemed to clean the air in his garage: "Having a six-foot pyramid in my garage has cleaned the air. Before building the pyramid, my dog slept in the garage and would use the floor as a toilet. Even after cleaning the mess it still left a distinct, highly unpleasant odor. I was not very happy at the prospects of having to put my pyramid in such a foul smelling room, but I had no choice. After five days the odor was gone and several friends commented on this. To this day the air in my garage remains fresh smelling."

One of the most amazing aspects of pyramid phenomena is that the results always seem to work for the benefit of mankind. One might anticipate that the forces would be neutral, and yet this doesn't seem to be the case. Plants such as poisonous mushrooms die while edible plants thrive, and there are sounds, colors, lights, and scents that can be used in a detrimental fashion against a person but these apparently do not occur within pyramids.

True, one man's poison may be another man's food, and we don't all have identical biochemical and bioelectrical needs. Despite these individual differences, we have never heard of anyone being harmed in any fashion because of pyramid energy. Yes, there have been those few people who have reported feeling uneasy or have developed a headache while being inside pyramids, but we are not at all sure that these early symptoms weren't necessary by way of some positive adjustment. Since there are individual differences, how do we account for the pyramid making this adjustment? We do not all "march to the same drummer" but our bodies and minds are able to select certain forces and frequencies that are beneficial and reject those that are not. This theory assumes that the body and mind gravitate toward health rather than illness, but many doctors, along with the mystics, agree that such is the case.

Another possible explanation is that intelligent forces are overseeing and guiding the work with pyramids. This is not so difficult to accept if we can believe that in the final analysis everything is consciousness. Undoubtedly pyramid energy could be abused—one could use it for selfish purposes, say, for power or to make money. And, yet, one can't help wondering if this was a person's goal whether the pyramid would continue to work for him.

We are told that everything in this world has its antithesis, so perhaps there is an anti-pyramid somewhere, or maybe just another shape that works against the welfare of mankind. If so, it would be nice to believe it will remain forever buried.

That pyramids designed after the Great Pyramid could possibly be used for evil purposes is something of which we have seen no evidence, and we remember our friend who tried to think depressing thoughts inside a pyramid and failed. It just may be that the pyramid is going to work for us, with or without our help.

7

Nectar of the Gods

Water, known to ancient man as one of the four elements of the universe, still remains a mystery after all these centuries. One of the primary sources of life, it is also the primary source of decay; it reacts both as a base and an acid. The first chemical formula taught a beginning high school chemistry student is that of water and yet the most profound scientific journals carry articles as to the nature of its structure. What is water? As easy to ask, what is life? Approximately sixty-five percent of the content of the human body is water, as is the surface of the world. Organic life originated in water and the very cells of our bodies are virtually marine organisms, actually tiny aquatic animals that can only exist when surrounded by water. Along with air, water must be present at all times if life is to be sustained.

In America but particularly in Europe today there are places famous for their water cures. Unless we can dismiss all the cases as spontaneous remission or psychosomatic, or attribute success to some other factor, cures are occurring. Is it simply a matter of flushing away the illness, or is some quality being instilled or drawn out of the water that makes it different from ordinary tap water? According to Yoga, not all water is equal, depending on the amount of prana or vital force it contains.

In a small volume, *The Practical Water Cure as Practiced in India and Other Oriental Countries,* Yogi Ramacharaka states, "Prana, which is contained in the water, may be transmuted and converted into other forms of energy, which will tend to invigorate and strengthen the human body, relieve physical disorders, and promote health and strength."

Holy water as something different from the ordinary brand is a tenet of religious belief. Is baptism transmuting human properties in a manner not limited to states of mind? Is there something more than minerals and heat in the water of popular hot-springs health resorts? What was it that Ponce de León heard about a fountain of youth? Maybe his source provided better details about its quality than they did as to its location. Is there something strange about the water bounded by the Bermuda Triangle? Is there something more in Rocky Mountain spring water than ample minerals? In what manner can a pyramid alter the structure of water in order that it might vitalize the skin when used as a lotion?

According to Lyall Watson in *Super Nature,* water is extremely flexible and the tenuous links between its atoms make it so susceptible that little external pressure can destroy the bonds and change its pattern. "Biological reactions must occur quickly and take place with very little expenditure of energy, so a trigger substance such as water is the ideal go-between," Watson states in pursuing his theory that water not only behaves in this manner inside a plant or animal, and that external forces not only change the form of water inside an organism, but that water by itself can be influenced in this way.

Giorgio Piccardi, director of the Institute for Physical Chemistry in Florence, found that certain chemical re-

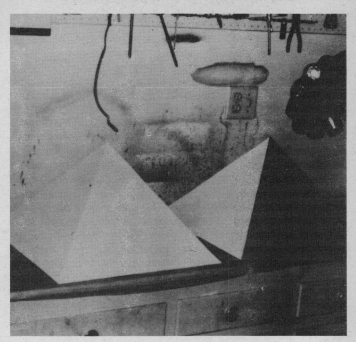

Pyramids used for storing water.

actions took place faster where there was a solar eruption and changes in the earth's magnetic field could be measured. Long-range changes plotted on a graph formed a curve exactly parallel to that for sunspot frequency in the eleven-year cycle. Piccardi's experiments on the precipitation of a chemical demonstrated that precipitation always took place at the normal speed beneath a copper screen. The screen evidently shielded the experiments from outside influences.

In *The Secret Power of Pyramids* we described our experiments with plant behavior inside and outside pyramid models. Both the experimental and the control plants were observed by means of time-lapse photography. The plants inside the pyramids went through a pronounced gyration by moving to the west, making an arc to the south, and swinging to the east every hour and fifty minutes. This pattern, with many plants and many pyramids, continued from the beginning of the experiment in the fall of 1971 until July 1974, when the plants stopped their dance, stood still for a few days, and then started moving in a north-south fashion. After about one week, however, the plants once again stopped their movement. At this writing, the plants remain more or less in suspended animation.

Perplexed by the sudden change of affairs, we explored all sorts of explanations, climatical, seasonal, environmental differences, and so on. However, it would now seem that the best explanation lies in relating the erratic behavior of the plants to the eleven-year low in sunspot activity. It is our hypothesis that as sunspot activity increases, the plants will again initiate their dance.

Yet the control plants outside the pyramids showed little movement at any time during the experimental period, and this leads us to believe that the pyramid amplifies the solar or cosmic influences on the plants. When an aluminum screen was placed on the west side of the plants they were inhibited in their movement. This seemed to indicate that the metal acted as a blocking agent or else was absorbing the influencing forces. In any case, our results parallel so closely those of Piccardi that it would seem reasonable to assume at this point that the property being influenced in the plant was the water content.

In *The Cosmic Clocks* Michel Gauquelin states, "At the National Center for Atmospheric Research of Boulder, Colorado, W. H. Fisher and his assistants have shown that the structure of water is extremely sensitive to electromagnetic fields. It is through the agency of such subtle fields of force that the cosmos modifies the properties of water."

Gauquelin proposes that Piccardi's experiments have vast implications and states, "Water is not only the liquid of our earth, it is also the liquid of our lives. Living organisms are exposed to the cosmos as the colloids in their laboratory beakers are. Cosmic forces act upon them through the mediation of the water contained in their bodies."

This research indicates that the structure of water is not static but dynamic and subject to a variety of influences. If we can believe the evidence of our research and that of others, water placed inside pyramids is altered in perceptible ways.

In *The Secret Power of Pyramids,* we mentioned that water kept in a pyramid for two weeks was used by Inez Pettit as a facial lotion. All other creams and cosmetics were dispensed with. After five weeks, friends started saying to her, "My, Inez, what are you using on your face? Your skin is just radiant."

Several people have told us that they have used pyramid water on their hair and were convinced it made their hair more manageable and softer. Ed Pettit's hair was thinning four years ago when he decided to treat it with pyramid water once a day. Now the barber has to thin his hair when cutting it. It has been reported that pyramid water stimulates hair growth if used as a rinse after shampoos.

Apparently water passes through a maturing process inside the pyramid. We have found that it reaches an optimal level of energy retention from ten days to two weeks. This was determined by testing the water on plants and measuring growth rate. Plastic, ceramic, or glass jars can be used and, apparently, are equally effective. Jars should be covered with something other than metal lids. Milk suspended from the apex of a large outside pyramid quickly soured when an aluminum screen was hung above it. It would appear that metal absorbs some of the energy spectrum. Since it takes several days for the metal to become saturated, when it no longer would act as a blocking agent, this duration of time is too long for the milk to retain its freshness. If this occurs with milk, we believe the water would also be affected in some manner by the presence of the metal. As with other objects, the jar should be placed under the apex of the pyramid. To be most effective, the jar should not take up too much of the volume of the pyramid. For example, the height of the pyramid should not be less than sixteen inches for treating one gallon of water. One can put up to eight gallons of water in a six-foot pyramid.

Water is one of the most effective and simple ways to conduct pyramid research. As the water apparently picks up the charge from the pyramid it can be used as a substitute pyramid. This allows the experimenter to conduct a great many tests at the same time and provides for more flexibility in testing. Undoubtedly, there are properties generated inside the pyramid that are not captured by the water, but nevertheless the range for using water instead of the pyramid directly is wide enough for many purposes.

Tests that can be run on oneself include drinking pyramid water instead of tap water; using the treated water as a facial lotion; shampooing the hair and/or rinsing it with pyramid water; brushing the teeth; and whatever else you can dream up for the water certainly is harmless. It can also be used as a balm for simple cuts and bruises. During the winter when the air is uncomfortably dry inside most homes, pans of pyramid water can be placed in safe places and allowed to evaporate, thus increasing the humidity and perhaps adding a freshening quality as well.

These tests, of course, are of a subjective nature and you may wish to have samples run on some of your treated water at a local laboratory. Two other samples should be tested at the same time: fresh water from the same source, and a control sample that was drawn at the same time as the experimental sample and has been kept in an identical container for the same length of time. Better yet, the control sample could be placed inside a box of equal volume and of the same material as the pyramid.

It might be interesting to see if friends can select the treated water from the tap water, but be sure they are cooled to the same temperature. Also, you might wish to run a test with your pets by setting out two pans of water, treated and untreated, and see which water they select.

Plant experiments can be easily carried out with treated water. Select four flower or vegetable seeds; put two each in identical pots filled with the same soil; water one with pyramid water and the other with regular water. Use exactly the same amount of water for each plant. Note which seeds germinate first and after the plants are one or two inches tall measure their growth two or three times a week. Use pyramid water on your house plants and, we have found, it keeps cut flowers longer than untreated water.

We haven't tried this one but it might be worthwhile to try pyramid water in aquariums; it should be healthy for marine life. If possible, you might wish to set up a second tank as a control and then if you could place baby something-or-the-others in the tanks you could check their growth rates.

Other experiments might include putting pyramid water in batteries, making enough treated water to soak in the bathtub occasionally as a vigorizing exercise, and improving the taste of beverages such as coffee and tea by using pyramid water. Water plays so many roles in

our lives that the number of possible experiments is end-
less. Another advantage of using water as a substitute
pyramid is that you can take a bottle of tonic with you
while traveling.

"The water from the pyramid seems to taste sweeter
and flows more smoothly into the stomach, releasing a
flow of energy into the solar plexus immediately," T.M.
of Denver, Colorado, states in a letter.

This is an interesting observation because the solar
plexus is viewed as one of the seven chakras, or energy
centers, in man, as described in the chapter, "The Serpent's Fire." The solar plexus is allegedly the recipient
of solar energy and in Yoga this center is associated with
fire. One of the definitions offered for pyramid is "fire
in the middle." The King's Chamber of the Great Pyramid is located in the middle of the pyramid's volume,
and the solar plexus is located in the middle of the human body. Fire and water have opposing qualities and
the "fire" in the middle of the pyramid may be, therefore, attracted to the water, generating a change.

"Prana permeates every drop of water, although in
varying degrees. Fresh running water contains a much
greater proportion of Prana than stagnant, still water.
Likewise water that has been contained in cisterns, tanks
or vessels is found to have parted with much of its
original store of Prana," Yogi Ramacharaka explains in
the book mentioned earlier.

Boiled and distilled water, according to Ramacharaka,
have lost much of their prana and he suggests that the
prana may be restored by passing the water through the
air, by pouring it from one vessel to another. This apparently aerates it.

"This water seems charged," people say to us. Almost
without fail they are able to detect which sample of
water has been kept inside a pyramid.

And Ramacharaka states that water "prana-ized will
be found to have a slightly invigorating and stimulating
effect absent from ordinary water. Persons who wish to
rid themselves of the desire for alcoholic stimulants will

find it much easier to do so if they will prana-ize their drinking water . . ."

Once again, the similarity in reported results between pyramid water and what Ramacharaka refers to as "prana-ized" water can be drawn from an account that we recently received in which a forty-year-old interior decorator stated: "I am an alcoholic. I could not accept this fact until I ran out of all other explanations. I am now working with a self-help group and on a special diet. But three weeks ago I started drinking pyramid water each time I yearned for liquid of high octane and I honestly believe this gives me relief."

In *The Guide to Pyramid Energy* Bill Kerrell and Kathy Goggin state, "Incidentally, some of our most interesting experiments have involved brine shrimp. We have hatched at least a dozen batches of these shrimp, each time with much the same results. Being sure that both the hatch under the pyramid and the control hatch are in environments as close to identical as possible, we have found that pyramid water and a pyramid over the test tank can greatly extend the lives of the shrimp.

"In almost every case, the control batch would live for a maximum of six or seven weeks, and usually less. In every case, the pyramid-treated shrimp would not only survive much longer but would grow two to three times larger . . ."

Elsewhere in the book, they remark, "Los Angeles, like many cities, has chlorinated water. After pyramid treatment, the water loses its chlorine taste and gains a decidedly sweeter flavor."

That water undergoes a structural change when subjected to an electrical charge was discovered more than two hundred years ago.

In 1747, a French abbot, Jean Antoine Nollet, carefully weighed daffodils, sparrows, pigeons, and cats and found they lost weight faster if electrified.

Fruits, meats, vegetables, and so on do lose weight and dehydrate inside pyramids. However, Nollet's experiments apparently were carried out on living plants and animals. The loss of weight by electrification can be applied to pyramid phenomena only in part. Living animals and plants do not lose weight as a result of being inside pyramids. However, a number of people have reported losing weight after spending some time inside pyramids but all of these persons wanted to lose weight. Perhaps it was positive thought on their part, but if we could assume that the change was due to pyramid phenomena, then we might ask if pyramids work toward balancing the body. Those who were not overweight did not lose weight, but this is not to say that the pyramid is a weight-reducing machine. There may be many people who want to drop a few pounds but have to find a way more strenuous than pyramid-sitting. We just don't know on this score, but we constantly hear from people that they feel better after using pyramids . . . so maybe they are happier and no longer express their frustrations in eating.

The pyramid seems to inject some beneficial property to water, for plants seem to thrive on it. "In all our comparative tests," Kerrell and Goggin state, "plants receiving pyramid-treated water showed hardier growth and looked generally healthier than the control plants receiving water straight from the tap . . . using pyramid-treated water for your cut flowers will extend their life. Blossoms and petals will not fall off while under the pyramid."

Credit is frequently given to animals as knowing what is best for their health and given a choice they invariably choose pyramid water.

It is said that Paracelsus gathered dew from plants during various configurations of the heavenly bodies, believing the water carried within it the energy of these planetary combinations.

A modern disciple of Paracelsus, Dr. Edward Bach, proposed that each dewdrop contained some of the properties of the plants on which it rested. He believed that certain plants held definite powers and that these powers were transmitted to the water on their surface. As collecting dewdrops can be an exacting trade at best, Bach decided instead to put the flowers in a bowl of fresh water.

Bach produced a total of thirty-eight remedies and many people in this country, but particularly in England, still swear by the "Bach Drops." A friend of ours in California has administered the drops for several years to growing numbers of patients at a health farm.

A. E. Powell explains in *The Etheric Double* that "the 'holy water' used in certain Christian churches affords a clear example of magnetization, water being very readily charged with magnetism. The instructions given in the Roman rite make it quite evident that the priest is required, first, to 'exorcise' the salt and water, i.e., to cleanse them from all objectionable influences, and then, making the sign of the cross, he is directed to 'bless' the elements, i.e., to pour his own magnetism into them, his will being directed to the purpose of driving away all evil thoughts and feelings."

One is reminded of Ramacharaka's reference to the combination of water and fire in Powell's statement, "It is worth noting that salt contains chlorine, a 'fiery' element, and hence the combination of water, the great solvent, with fire the great consumer, is highly effective as a cleansing agent."

"Precisely similar ideas underlie many other ceremonies in the Christian Church: such as baptism, in which the water is blessed and the sign of the cross made over it . . . In the Eucharist, the wine has a very powerful influence upon the higher astral levels, while the water sends out etheric vibrations." In discussing the sprinkling of the holy water on the head, Powell explains, "In addition the magnetized water, as it touches the forehead, sets violently in vibration the etheric matter, stimulates the brain, and through the pituitary body affects the astral body, and through that the material body."

If water is the perfect "triggering" medium, as Lyall Watson states, then it would seem to serve as an excellent storing agent for pyramid energy. It is not too likely, however, that any one medium can totally capture all of the powers of the pyramid . . . unless that medium is man who alone, we are told, contains all expressionable levels of the universe.

8

Beyond Drugs

About one hundred and twenty-five years ago the Boston physician Oliver Wendell Holmes wrote about the unconscious mind—many years before Freud initiated his investigations of the subject. Holmes experimented on himself with the mental sensations induced by inhaling ether, and he published the following account:

"I once inhaled a pretty full dose of ether, with the determination to put on record, at the earliest moment of regaining consciousness, the thought that I should find uppermost in my mind. The mighty music of the triumphal march into nothingness reverberated through my brain, and filled me with a sense of infinite possibilities, which made me an archangel for the moment. The veil of eternity was lifted. The one great truth which underlies all human experience, and is the key to all the mysteries that philosophy has sought in vain to solve, flashed on me in a sudden revelation. Henceforth, all was clear: a few words had lifted my intelligence to the level of the knowledge of the cherubim. As my natural condition returned . . . I wrote . . . the all embracing truth still glimmering in my consciousness. The words were these (children may smile; the wise will ponder): 'A strong smell of turpentine prevails throughout.' "

The drug scene has been with us for some time now and of recent years the psychedelics, ranging from acid to airplane glue and dried banana peels, have made quite an impact on our culture. The implications of a movement involving directly an estimated fifty percent of our young people are vast and complex and certainly outside the thrust of this book. It is mentioned here, however, because we have been hearing about one solution to the drug problem. More than a few young people have visited, called, and written to us saying that after they started spending some time in pyramids they lost their interest in drugs. "I didn't give them up; they gave me up" is a typical statement and it seems to imply that this change of affairs is something that happens rather than occurring by design. Of course, there may have been strong unconscious feelings about getting off drugs, but most of the youngsters we have talked with have stated that they had no intentions of abandoning their chemical highs in favor of pyramid sitting. It was to serve only as an adjunct.

A seventeen-year-old male high school senior in Galveston, Texas, wrote to us:

"I tried LSD several times but got flashbacks and didn't like it. Gave that up but was really heavy on pot for more than a year. Read your book *The Secret Power of Pyramids* and decided to build one. I put it up in my bedroom and started sleeping in it. Pot at first seemed good inside the pyramid, then the effect began fading off. Then I found I couldn't get high on pot anymore, but discovered I didn't need it. Seem to get better feeling, almost high just inside pyramid. I now have money for other things."

Tim Leary, the high priest of psychedelia, once stated that LSD should be used to bring the user beyond the need for it. The history of drug use doesn't seem to bear out this aphorism, but there are some rather exciting highs around serving as alternatives to drugs.

All highs are not equal, as all alternative states of consciousness are not samadhi. There apparently are some definitive differences between transitory and distorted glimpses into other than usual corners of the mind and elevated states of consciousness realized through effort and growth. There likely are some parallels, for in both instances cortical activity has been minimized and other aspects of the mind have come into play. Some of the emotional activity, sensitivity, and visual acuity are similar, for some of the same ground is being crossed. But the map is not the journey and a peek in the window is not the same at all as living in the room. Closer examination of the drug experience and the true mystical experience may provide us some insight as to why pyramid builders might healthfully and sanely replace drug pushers.

In *Higher Consciousness* the following question is directed to Gopi Krishna: "What are the essential characteristics of the genuine mystical experience and how can you distinguish it from the experiences caused by mind-altering drugs such as mescalin, hashish, LSD?"

He answers: "In the first place, mystical experience is overwhelming in a way that transforms the personality . . . It is disappointing that there still persists a belief that the altered states of consciousness, brought about by taking drugs like hashish or LSD, correspond in any way to the genuine mystical experience. It should be enough to say that though the latter is inexpressible, one can convey a distant picture by describing it as the highest perfection of grace, beauty, grandeur, harmony, peace, love, rapture, wonder, and happiness, all combined in such an intense degree that the mind may swoon at the stupendous impact of the ecstasy. The drug experience, on the other hand, is exciting and disorienting rather than inspiring. It is not integrated with the normal consciousness and launches the ego into sensational fantasies and distorted perceptions, tending to create addiction and craving rather than creative transformation.

"In genuine mystical experience there is often a permanent effect on the mind that has a transforming action on the whole of life. It leads to unshakable belief in the existence of God . . ."

William James spoke of the drug experiences in *Varieties of Religious Experience:* "Nitrous oxide, when sufficiently diluted with air, stimulates the mystical consciousness in an extraordinary degree. Depth beyond depth of truth seems revealed to the inhaler. This truth fades out, however, or escapes, at the moment of coming to; and if any words remain over in which it seemed to clothe itself, they prove to be of the veriest nonsense . . ."

We have discussed various maps of consciousness in previous chapters and they need not be repeated here. In reference to those maps, however, we might speculate that drugs tend to reduce the efficiency of the cerebral reducing valve, as Huxley calls it, and "when the brain runs out of sugar, the undernourished ego grows weak, can't be bothered to undertake the necessary chores, and loses all interest in those spatial and temporal relationships which mean so much to an organism bent on getting on in the world . . ."

With the rational mind out of gear, and awareness shifted to the right hemisphere, the observer can function on intuitive or theta levels and from this vantage point the world is less logical but exceedingly more glorious. "If the doors of perception were cleansed, every thing would appear to man as it is, infinite," William Blake propounded. The problem, of course, is what constitutes "cleansed." Where drugs are used as the fuel for launching oneself into inner space, the chemical explosion in the mind fails to bring off the transmutation and one plunges earthward again wide-eyed but untranscended. Something more is required.

"The Vedantists say that one may stumble into superconscious sporadically, without the previous discipline, but is then impure," William James states. "Their test of its purity, like our test of religion's value, is empirical: its fruits must be good for life. When a man comes out of Samadhi, they assure us that he remains 'enlightened, a sage, a prophet, a saint, his whole character changed, his life changed, illumined.' "

And Vivekananda states in *Raja Yoga:* "That the mind itself has a higher state of existence, beyond reason, a superconscious state, and that when the mind gets to that higher state, then this knowledge beyond reasoning comes . . . Then the Truth shines in its full effulgence, and we know ourselves—for Samadhi lies potential in us all—for what we truly are, free, immortal, omnipotent, loosed from the finite . . ."

As a staff member of the attorney general's office of Kansas, serving as director of Juvenile and Youth Affairs, and as a staff member of the Department of Preventive Psychiatry of the Menninger Foundation for a number of years, I (Schul) had the opportunity to work with persons with drug problems. For a time I endeavored to teach meditation to young addicts who frequented Carriage House, a walk-in place of counseling sponsored by the Menninger Foundation. It would be too positive a statement to say that none of these individuals gained from their drug experiences. It is quite likely some insights were gained, but I have never known an individual who ever became more ingenuous, more inventive, a better writer or artist, or the proud possessor of the human virtues described by Krishna, James, Vivekananda, and others because of drugs. I have seen artists paint differently because of drugs but not in my opinion better, although there may be art critics who will disagree with me. Creative expression was not one of Richard Alpert's strong points during his drug heydays. This had to wait until he was kicked out of Harvard, along with Tim Leary, and went to India where he discovered true mystical states and changed his name to Baba Ram Das.

We have had some success with persons giving up drugs

after becoming involved in meditation. The Transcendental Meditation people have made some very impressive inroads on this score, and several studies have now been made of this phenomenon.

The field of biofeedback has reported similar successes, and now we are beginning to hear that spending time in pyramids can accomplish much the same thing.

"I've constructed pyramids for a number of young people and several of them have told me later that they had given up drugs," Joe Wall, Milwaukee, told us. "They were obviously more stable and seem to be much happier and have some direction in their lives."

Meditation, biofeedback, experiencing pyramid space seem to serve the purpose of promoting relaxation, inner scanning, and the directing of consciousness away from external stimuli, the ego, and toward higher levels of the mind.

Quite a parade of people have come to our place and asked if they could sit for a while in one of the pyramids. I (Pettit) encourage them to do so and I'm amazed how many people then build their own pyramids. It would be hard to imagine them doing this if they didn't experience something different about it.

Sleep deprivation and sensory deprivation initiate hallucinations of some magnitude, creating scenes and a parade of figures that for all the world smack of reality to their creator. But when they die, their immortality rests with a few vague fragments in the dreamer's mind and never again are they resurrected. Even here, there is the possibility that one can track his phantoms beyond their forms and enter into transcendental states, but this accomplishment requires the talents of someone who has learned the secret of not getting caught up in visual phenomena.

Undoubtedly there are many ways to see the world—car, ship, plane, on foot, through a telescope, microscope—and each view will present its own reality, or, perhaps more accurately, its portion of reality. It would be difficult to decipher which perspective is the best or the most accurate.

Yet, there are ways, on the other hand, to determine the validity, the value, of an experience. The final test, it would seem, is the manner in which an experience has influenced a person's life. Whereas a person who is blind may experience the world differently from someone with vision, as will an individual who has clairvoyant sight, the question nevertheless always comes back to what influence the experience has had on the individual himself. Is this person any better, kinder, happier, stronger, compassionate, wiser, because of the experience? In the end what a person is tells us all we need to know about the value of the influences in his life.

A clairvoyant looks at a drug user and sees patches of burned and frayed edges in his aura; he looks at someone who practices meditation and sees a healthy, bright aura, and this is also true of someone who has been using a pyramid. This should tell us something about approaches. To our knowledge, none of the world's great teachers ever arrived at their elevated states through chemical magic. They quite likely, however, made use of the beneficial forces of nature, and they probably were able to select these forces by the type of field they radiated. The role played by various food substances in man's evolution and the manner in which pyramids affect these items will be described in the chapter "Nutritional Alchemy."

We have become so alarmed at human behavior of late that there has been more and more discussion of operant engineering—the use of technology to mold human beings —that remote control of the brain with electrical probes, genetic engineering, pharmacological alteration of personality, and the control of behavior with electronic surveillance devices. The public has become so concerned that Harvard psychologist B. F. Skinner's *Beyond Freedom and Dignity,* which advocates systematic behavior control as the solution to social problems, reached bestseller status. And in *Biofeedback* Marvin Karlins and Lewis Andrews note, "At the 1971 meeting of the

American Psychological Association, its president, Kenneth Clark, a professor at the City University of New York . . . made national headlines when he told delegates that antihostility drugs should be administered to political and military leaders to 'diminish their emotional propensities to respond to an international crisis by initiating a nuclear war.' Clark also suggested wider use of similar drugs by lesser officials and even civilians."

Frightening? Yes—especially if one remembers Huxley's prophecies in *Brave New World* and finds them coming true with startling precision. But there are positive alternatives . . . choices resting where they have always been, that self-awareness and control are prerequisites to social control. Self-growth approaches such as meditation are important because they place the power for change and control in the hands of the individual, not with an external authority. If we survive long enough, we will see the Skinners forgotten in the wake of such movements as Transcendental Meditation.

We would like to believe that pyramid research contributes to the latter movement. We have described how experiencing pyramid space contributes to relaxation, feelings of inner poise, vitality, creativity, and meditation, and the chapters on "The Healing Phenomenon" and "The Dweller Within" discuss the use of pyramids in physical and mental healing. We are not saying that living and working in pyramids will answer all the world's problems but we do feel that pyramids may make a contribution to the solutions. When more than one mother tells us her child is less hyperactive and more contented after spending some time in a pyramid, and when people tell us that feelings of hostility are impossible to generate inside pyramids, we believe the matter warrants more than a passing glance.

9

The Healing Phenomenon—I

"I can't remember when I've had this much unin-
terrupted sleep during the night. The nerves that were
damaged in my arm usually start throbbing after I'm in
bed a short time. It's been that way for months. Then I
started sitting for a while each day in a pyramid—not
with any real faith but out of desperation. I was willing
to try anything. What happened, I have no idea, but the
pain has lessened considerably and last night I slept for
eight straight hours."

"I've suffered from sinus congestion for years, at times
severely. I doubt that there is any such thing as a cure.
But I can tell you this: When my head gets stuffy, I head
for my pyramid and the frequencies, or whatever it is,
opens up my sinus cavities."

"You say you're really not sure why the pyramid works
and I say, 'Who cares as long as it does.' I'll leave that
discovery to the scientists and in the meantime I'll use
mine to get rid of my backache."

Headaches, arthritis, broken bones, stomach disorders
. . . we have a stack of reports several inches thick from
persons who have written us about some kind of healing
experience, relief of pain, and the feeling of greater
vitality and strength which they attribute to the use of
pyramids. What does this mean? Are we to believe that
pyramids will cure all our physical and mental ills? It
would be nice to so believe. A few pieces of wood are a
bit cheaper than the going rates for doctors and hospitals.
But such faith might be asking too much of impossible
dreams.

Needless to say, we are more likely to hear from
those who experience results than from those who don't.
All of us have known persons who can't seem to register
beneficial health results under any circumstances. They
have tried a host of physicians—allopaths or medical
doctors, osteopaths, chiropractors, psychiatrists, naturo-
paths, homeopaths—clinics, cures, exercises, pills, herbs,
food supplements, and just about everything else natural
or invented by the mind of man. All to no avial.

We have to assume that in such cases their problems
are not physical in origin and therefore do not yield to
physical applications. They may not be psychological
either, in the traditional sense, and to group them under
the category of psychosomatic illnesses would be too
simplistic unless we define the term very broadly. Such a
definition would include those causes stemming from the
mind but other than those struggles with unconscious fears,
motivations, and so on.

If, indeed, the pyramid does generate a force field that
contributes to healing, it may not apply to some persons
for the same reasons that physicians have been unable to
help. The conclusion that one must reach is that all of
these approaches, including pyramids, have simply not
penetrated to the cause of the disease or the affliction.
This is the problem that one runs into when expecting to
find simple answers to complex conditions. Disease cannot
be seen as just a bug that has penetrated a physical body
or as an illness that is "all in one's head."

With the advent of psychology and the later defining of psychosomatic illnesses we began to realize that the cause of illness can be as readily mental as physical with the symptoms equally visible in the physical body. The application of physical approaches to causes that are mental fails to yield results and vice versa. In the early part of this century it was learned how important it was for man to have a diet balanced in vitamins and minerals. If these nutrients were balanced, he might still have problems if not producing the necessary enzymes for digestion, or if the body's chemical regulators, the hormones, were not being properly produced and utilized. Further, it was discovered that some people—for reasons still unknown—develop reactions to some foods and end up with very serious allergies of the central nervous system. Thus everything mechanical about the body could be in good operating form and nothing haunting the unconscious mind, but unless the vitamins, minerals, protein, carbohydrates, enzymes, hormones, and so on were fulfilling their roles and not causing any nervous disorders, health could not be maintained.

By this time, then, medicine was concerned with physical, mechanical, psychological, and biochemical factors, all equally capable of producing ill health in the physical body. In recent years more and more attention has been focused on another factor. With the development of highly sensitive instruments another dimension of the human system was discovered—the electrical. It was found that the body not only has nerve current, blood flow, lymph circulation, but an electrical current related to but also separate from the other systems. This dimension came under closer scrutiny with the popularization of acupuncture in this and other Western countries. Mystics had talked about the electrical flow within and immediately surrounding the body for centuries but they had to await the entry of acupuncture into Western medicine and the development of Kirlian photography for their offerings to be appreciated. In Kirlian, or high-frequency, photography an electrical current is used instead of light to expose film. When high-frequency current is applied to a plate and film and a picture taken of some part of the body, what is seen on the developed film is a corona or electrical changes according to physical, emotional, and mental states and the process is now being researched as a new diagnostic tool.

Added to the above factors, then, was the bioelectrical dimension, and this meant that along with everything else the electrical or electromagnetic ingredient in the cells, tissue, muscle, blood, organs, and so on would also have to be in good working order for good health.

As it became more and more evident that all of the dimensions of the body were related, integrated, and involved in health, many doctors started talking about the holistic approach to man, or medicine of the whole person. A sufficient number of physicians, osteopaths, and chiropractors have become interested in the holistic approach to indicate a trend. We have attended several national medical conferences on the holistic theme during the past few years and have noticed a growing participation on the part of eminent medical scientists.

The last such conference we attended was the First Congress on Integrative Medicine, sponsored by the Academy of Parapsychology and Medicine and held in Tucson, Arizona, October 8–10, 1975. Renowned medical scientists such as Dr. Roy Menninger, president of the Menninger Foundation; Dr. Malcolm Todd, 1974–1975 president of the American Medical Association; and Dr. Hans Selye, director of the Institute of Experimental Medicine and Surgery at the University of Montreal and internationally recognized authority on stress, appeared on the program and urged their medical colleagues to think in terms of treating the whole person and not just a disease.

Still, the dimensions of medicine do not end here. There is a growing number of scientists and informed laymen who are now saying that to truly take the holistic approach another factor must be included—the spiritual one. Theologians have said this for a long time but now they have been joined by the scientists, and suddenly science, long held by some to be the antithesis of religion, has become its apostle.

Until the advent of the unified-field theory—which views everything in the universe as some form of energy or further, still, as consciousness—the Western scientific concepts of matter did not provide for the intrusion of spirit into any kind of relationship with physical substance. Spirit did not exist within the nomenclature of the scientist. If he spoke of it at all, he put on a different hat to do so. He could not deal with such matters as spiritual healing or the efficacy of prayer, for he had found no evidence of a bridge between spirit and matter, no medium through which one could influence the other. While psychology and the study of psychosomatic diseases had clearly demonstrated the effects of nonmaterial thoughts and feelings on the physical body, mental and emotional influences were seen as chemical components.

For centuries clairvoyants and mystics have described the aura or etheric quality permeating and surrounding all life forms and particularly man. These etherical or electrical properties they claimed to be of great importance in understanding life. The individual's physical, emotional, mental, and spiritual states, they said, were reflected in the aura and largely determined the state of health.

Yet within the scientific disciplines auras had little place where hard data alone was respected. The visions of the mystics were ignored in an arena where only mechanical and chemical principles were allowed. But the development of more sophisticated instruments, due in large part to the demands of the space age, started introducing additional dimensions of life into view, and that which was nonexistent suddenly became substance worthy of investigation.

The bridge between matter and spirit had been constructed. Within a unified field theory, energy became the basis of all life, whether viewed in solid or spirit form. When it was discovered that the energy field could be manipulated by thought, consciousness became the principal agent of change. The power of mind over matter suddenly became one of those facts scientists are so fond of and they had to live with it. The fields of psychology and psychosomatic causes gained new reality bases, and psychologists, biologists, chemists, physicists, and theologians found themselves in the same room talking about the spiritual factor in healing. The subject, it would seem, was inevitable—the natural result of the chain of events. With consciousness in the central position of common denominator, value systems, attitudes, all those qualities particularly human no longer could be exiled from the laboratory. Physics recognized awareness; psychology altered its position from the mechanical to the humanistic and even the transpersonal; and medicine moved toward the holistic. Science and religion had vindicated each other.

Rather than being far afield from pyramids and healing, this examination of developments in science and medicine has a direct bearing on our understanding of pyramid phenomena. It not only illustrates why pyramid research has captured the attention of the public but, hopefully, offers an explanation why many scientists view the findings not as curious, isolated phenomena but as another arena in which to explore energy fields.

There is another aspect of the cause and effect of illness that may have some bearing on why some people have such a difficult time discovering the causes of their health problems. This factor takes a philosophical position as to the nature of disease. Disease or afflictions can be viewed as serving an underlying purpose. They are part of a design and fulfill a role in man's development. It is not that one resigns himself to illness or that it is something to be encouraged. Rather, illness is to be overcome but only with the advent of learning and growth. When the knowledge has been gained, the cause has been satisfied and the symptoms disappear. Not only is this one of the concepts of illness as viewed in Eastern medicine today, but as one of the tenets of the ancient mystery schools it has a bearing on the beliefs of the builders of the Great Pyramid.

Eastern medicine holds to the belief that everything that happens is for the purpose of learning and this includes disease. If a person is ill, it is because he has something to learn. Health and disease are closely tied to the concept of karma. Karma is closely identified to the Christian idea that one reaps what one sows. However, the law of karma is seen as fulfilling the need for balance and growth: what has not been done must be done; what has not been learned must be learned if man is eventually to become perfect. Within this view, disease or afflictions do not occur because of chaotic or nonintelligent conditions. Instead everything has a purpose and a design, and while a germ might be the physical cause of disease, the primary cause might be a karmic one. The ultimate responsibility for health rests with each person. While the physician can treat the physical effect, the individual is responsible for getting at the cause, the reason for the disease.

While most Western medical scientists are not prepared to include the law of karma as one of the essential components of health and disease, there is a growing trend toward seeing man as having physical, emotional, mental, and spiritual dimensions and not being just a mechanical-chemical composite. The implication of this approach is that man's health or lack of it involves his complete being—physical, chemical, electrical, emotional, mental, and spiritual—and to administer to only one aspect is to deal with effects but not causes.

All of this is tantamount to explaining that it is no longer acceptable within either Western or Eastern medicine to assume that illness is so simple that a pill, a stroke of the knife, a heating pad, a good thought, an electrical charge, or any other single approach is going to be anywhere close to a complete answer.

For anyone to imagine that sitting in or using pyramids in some fashion justifies tearing up health-insurance papers is to indulge in fantasy. But it would also be unrealistic, it would seem, to ignore the evidence of something going on inside the pyramid that contributes to healing. The pyramid may not be the answer but it may help to provide some answers.

Dr. William McGarey is director of the A.R.E. clinic (Association for Research and Enlightenment) in Phoenix, Arizona. For many years he has researched and applied the medical principles of Edgar Cayce, the sleeping prophet who gave thousands of medical readings before his death in 1945. One remedy that he has found a wide use for is castor-oil packs. He uses them for a variety of both internal and external medical problems. Dr. McGarey has found that they work very well but he makes a rather interesting observation regarding the success of the packs: he notes that they work best "when the patient has a castor-oil consciousness." What we think we hear Dr. McGarey saying is that health is really a state of consciousness on some level. This does not mean that anything will work as long as you have faith in it, but it does imply that "as a man thinketh in his heart, so is he," that our world, including our bodies, is a mental construct. This goes back to what Dr. Elmer Green stated: "All of the body is in the mind, but not all of the mind is in the body."

During the spring of 1975 we attended the interdisciplinary conferences on "The Psychology of Consciousness and Suggestology" sponsored by Pepperdine University of Los Angeles. One of the speakers was Dr. Georgi Lozanov, director of both the Institute for Parapsychology and the Institute for Suggestology in Bulgaria and the pioneer of parapsychology in that country. Dr. Lozanov told the conference that by using his principles of suggestology subjects were able to perform tasks beyond their presumed talents because they were convinced that they could. Such feats would seem to indicate that the human mind is really unlimited.

When we started our research with pyramids, we did not anticipate that healing or the relief of pain would become an issue. We had not given it any thought. The discovery that sitting in pyramids would relieve aches and pains was largely by accident. When the unexpected happened, we tried it again. When it happened the second time, we continued to test. The letters we have received from people also describe these kinds of discoveries. One of our first experiences with healing had to do with a gerbil. We put the small rodent in her cage under a pyramid as we were curious to see how she would fare. Shortly after this she lacerated her face rather badly on the cage, but without treatment of any kind the cut quickly healed and left no scar. We were sure there was something unusual about this. Thereafter, any cut or bruise we received was treated either by sitting inside a pyramid or placing the injured member, such as a hand, under a smaller pyramid for a little while each day. Some of these experiences will be described later.

We believe these experiences should be shared with others, and this is the spirit in which people have contacted us about their experiences. This is the way we learn. On the other hand, for several reasons, we can't recommend pyramid use to someone who approaches us with a medical problem. We are not licensed to practice medicine and if we were to suggest to that person to try the pyramid we might influence him to avoid needed medical assistance. The only responsible suggestion we can make is that if medical aid is indicated, it should be obtained. Our hope is that pyramid research can contribute to the knowledge of the human system and how it functions and not in any sense distract from it or cause anyone to exercise bad judgment in regard to his health. Our experiences, the cases cited, the letters quoted, and the interpretations we offer on the following pages in light of scientific findings should be considered in the spirit of research and discovery. Our working hypotheses and the conclusions we may draw or allude to from time to time are not for a moment to be construed as any kind of final word on the subject. Nor should the reader entertain the thought that this will be our position a year or five years from now. It would be discouraging to imagine that we would learn nothing during that period of time.

Knowledge in the fields of medicine, biology, psychology, physics, and so on is mushrooming so rapidly that anything written is almost obsolete by the time it is printed. Research is moving that fast. No one, researcher or observer, can afford the complacency to accept today's conclusion on an issue as an established fact. Facts are the luxury of the omnipotent mind; none of the scientists we know of can qualify. So we are wiser if we approach so-called facts with the qualifying addendum "This is as it appears today." Anyone choosing to be more definite or positive is flirting with the truth.

What is it that we have learned to date about the healing powers of pyramids? First of all, we do not know for certain that pyramids help in the healing process. We have collected many reports, however, that pain is eased or eliminated and healing takes place in less than normal time. The healing may be coincidental, but this is doubtful. More and more physical and mental problems are being classified as psychosomatic. This might be expected, since the new medicine, along with the new physics, is moving away from the particle theory of substance to the unified-field theory of energy and now even toying with the idea that all is consciousness. Using the model of the world as consciousness it is easy to understand why some doctors are saying that all physical and mental problems are psychosomatic.

But translating psychosomatic as it is usually used means those health problems that are not traceable to organic causes. We have no way of knowing if pyramid healings occur only with psychosomatic problems, but we would assume that this classification does not apply to lacerations, bruises, and so on. We would also find it difficult to apply the label of psychosomatic to animals and we have received many reports relating to various pets.

Earlier we discussed the multifaceted nature of health and disease. If, then, disease can enter the body at the physical, chemical, electrical, emotional, mental, or spiritual level, and the pyramid can alleviate the problem, at what level does it accomplish this? "Phenomena is occurring in healing for which we have no diagnosis— no way of describing it—phenomena we must understand if medicine is going to meet the demands being made of it today," Dr. Roy Menninger stated in his keynote address to the First Congress on Integrative Medicine.

Faced with the problem as stated by the president of the Menninger Foundation, we can try to decipher at what level the pyramid may work by surveying some of the phenomena. The pyramid seems to alter organic structures judging from its affect on cuts, food products, water, and metals. The application may be at the physical or chemical level. Since the force field generated or amplified inside the pyramid appears to have electromagnetic qualities, the effect produced may be at the bioelectrical level. Inasmuch as persons experiencing pyramid space feel more contented, tranquil, and even lose their hostilities, the input may be at the emotional level. Since many persons sitting or meditating inside pyramids experience altered and elevated states of consciousness, the application may be of a mental nature. Feelings of sensitivity beyond the sensual, of heightened awareness above the rational, and the impressions of oneness may indicate a spiritual source of influence.

The pyramid gives every indication of working at all seven levels of the human system as given earlier— physical, etheric, astral, lower mind, higher mind, soul, and spirit. That is one way of looking at it. Another way, however, is by means of the consciousness-is-everything model. All other expressions—physical, chemical, electrical, and so on—are simply appearances on the face of consciousness. Everything is one, the great Indian sage Sri Aurobindo said, and it matters little whether one considers everything as physical matter with spirit as its most rarified form or as spirit with physical matter being its most densified form. Accepting this schematic as the most accurate one, we divide the human system into various levels not because that's the way it is but because this is the only way our human minds can comprehend it. The divisions are arbitrary, not actual, according to this scheme.

"Spirit" within the seven-level division represents omnipotence or the Universal Mind. In the final analysis if this is all there is, then everything else is a thought within the Universal Mind, or what Vedanta calls the Dream of Brahma. According to this ideology, everything has its origin and its existence within the Universal Mind. Everything has a design and purpose as conceived by That which thinks it. All disease, then, has a spiritual origin, and we find one of our most eminent physicists, Dr. William Tiller of Stanford University, saying exactly this:

"All illness has its origin in a disharmony between the mind and spirit levels of the entity and that of the universal pattern for the entity. Permanent healing and wholeness require that harmony with the universal pattern exist at the mind and spirit levels. Thus, healing at the physical or even the etheric level is only temporary if the basic pattern at the mind and spirit level remains unchanged."

"When one is attuned, he is in touch with the spiritual sources of energy," Dr. Marshall Spangler, internationally recognized authority on computer-aided medical diagnosis, stated at the conference on "The Psychology of Consciousness and Suggestology," mentioned earlier.

His son, David, educator and writer, echoed this theme when he told the conference, "Health may be defined as wholeness that embodies an individual's relationship to himself and in a consciousness that perceives our planet as one related, living system."

If all disease has a spiritual origin, then it would seem to follow that it could be alleviated at that level. This is apparently the level at which spiritual healing takes place, but in order for change to become a reality the individual has to be spiritually aware in order to benefit from the change, otherwise the disease must be intercepted at some stage below this. According to Eastern traditions, the law of karma applies here. The disease or affliction is established because there is something in the person's life that requires correction or a process of learning. If the spiritual insight can be gained and the necessary changes made, then the disease need not be experienced at any other level. Occasionally one hears about the spontaneous remission of a disease. According to this tradition, this occurs when the lesson involved has been learned; the cause is removed and the effect follows. This does not necessarily occur at the conscious level. It is believed that learning can take place in other than the conscious domain, although the experience will likely be understood by the conscious mind at some point in the person's development.

If the affliction is not corrected at the higher levels of the mind, it progresses downward, so to speak, through the lower levels of the mind, astral and etheric envelopes to be eventually materialized in the physical body. At any point along the way, however, the illness can be intercepted and eliminated if sufficient knowledge and will are applied. It is at the etheric level, for example, that psychic healing is believed to take place. At this point, the disease has not become manifested within the physical body. However, since the etheric envelope does have some physical density and is sometimes referred to as the aura, it can be seen by clairvoyants. Such individuals claim they can see the presence of illness in the aura and depending upon its color, intensity, and location can predict the kind of illness that will soon be experienced in the body. Dr. Norman Shealy, associate clinical professor at both the University of Minesota and the University of Wisconsin, has been appearing at medical conferences around the country and urging medical practitioners to make greater use of clairvoyant diagnosticians. He cites a five-year study in which clairvoyant diagnosticians were more accurate than medically trained ones.

The etheric envelope when viewed by a clairvoyant and to some extent at least in Kirlian photography reveals changes in its structure, intensity, and coloring according to the subject's health. Successful treatment of a problem is then reflected in the aura usually before it is experienced in the body. Dr. Hugh Riordan, a Wichita, Kansas, psychiatrist who practices acupuncture and is researching the Kirlian process as a diagnostic tool, demonstrated this concept for us. Kirlian photos first were taken of our fingerpads. One of us then told him that he was suffering from a low back pain. The pain was then treated by auricular therapy or ear acupuncture and the pain was relieved. Again a Kirlian photo was taken and it was quite easy, even for a layman, to see the difference in the corona pattern.

Both clairvoyants and Kirlian photography have been used to observe the change in the auric radiation resulting from energy transferred from a healer to a patient. Such changes in the etheric or electrical field around the human body as a result of successful treatment by a healer indicate that it is at this level that psychic healing and the method known as the laying-on-of-hands takes place. The healer transfers energy from his own body to the energy-electrical field of the patient. The energy-electrical envelope then materializes changes in the physical body. Measurements of human energy fields will be discussed in the chapter on experiments. However, we might note here that methods sometimes referred to as magnetic healing, polarity therapy, balancing of energy fields, and the acupuncture concept of eliminating blockages in the energy channels or meridians likely apply to the etheric dimension of the human system.

Inasmuch as we seem to be principally concerned with energy force fields of some nature with pyramids, it appears likely that it is also at the etheric level that much of the influence of the forces within the pyramid apply. While some of the pyramid's channeling may enter the human system at levels above the etheric, much of the healing phenomena is similar to that of psychic healing, magnetic healing, laying-on-of-hands, acupuncture, and so on. We should explain, however, that healing probably never takes place at a single level. Following our earlier argument, permanent healing will not take place at all unless the cause for the illness has been eliminated. One way of looking at the matter is that the emphasis might be at a particular level—physical, mental, and so on—with the other levels being indirectly involved.

The seven principles of man "interpenetrate each other. They, through the polarity principle, form atoms and molecules and configurations of these. One can apply the metaphysical principle, 'As above, so below; as below, so above,' and realize that what we see in the physical may be used as a model and this same kind of modelling understanding may be extrapolated through the other levels of substance, differing somewhat in detail from the physical, and we may begin conceptually to grapple with these other levels," Dr. Tiller stated during the symposium on "Dimensions of Healing," held at Stanford University, September 30–October 3, 1972. He continued, "The substances interpenetrate, and their relationship may be visualized by considering the situation in our own bodies. To visualize our seven bodies, think of seven transparent sheets of paper and, on these sheets, using particular pens of different colors, draw circuitry of some color on one, and on another draw circuitry of another color, and so on through the seven colors. Then, put these sheets all together and look through them, and you will see an organization of substance at the various levels within the bodies of the man . . ."

Dr. Tiller then explained to the gathering how the levels interact: "In general, these substances do not interact too strongly. However, they can be brought into interaction with each other through the agency of the mind, and it is really at the point of mind that one can bring about changes in the organization of structure in these various levels of substance. That is, through mind forces, one can create a pattern, and that pattern then acts as a force field which applies to the next level of substance. In turn, that force field is a force for organizing the atoms and molecules into configurations at that level of substance. That pattern of substance at the etheric level, then, is in a particular state of organization and it has its own radiation field—its own force field, if you like—and that force field, then, is a field for the organization of matter at the next level of substance—the physical level of substance . . . Here we see something that I have chosen to call the 'ratchet' effect; one can see an action beginning at the mind level and working its way down through to produce an effect on the physical level (and vice versa)."

Sister Justa Smith believes that healing takes place within the body and that all that the physician, healer, and, in our case, the pyramid can do is assist in the process.

Speaking at the same symposium as Dr. Tiller, Dr. Smith told the participants:

"Most thinking people today will accept the fact that there is 'something' within the body which controls the healing process, growth, repair and so forth. These functions take place without action of the conscious mind. No matter the number of degrees held by the physician, he is unable to do more than approximate the ends of a fractured bone and must depend upon the innate intelligence of the patient's body to effect the actual repair process. No disease has ever been cured by any practitioner of healing. He does many things to assist in the healing process of the body, but in the final analysis, it is that 'intelligence within' that makes the actual correction. No one has a suitable, scientific explanation of this 'something' within each of us which distinguishes the living from the dead. Volumes would be wasted trying to explain and prove innate intelligence, for this is beyond finite knowledge. It is much more rewarding to attempt to find the mechanism by which the body functions, recognizing full well that we are not in any position to make claims for total knowledge of human function and do not have all the answers to the perplexing questions of life, health and disease."

And pyramid space raises its own set of perplexing questions of life, health and disease. As with the other phenomena produced by its own unique inner space, the pyramid makes great demands on our understanding in order for us to piece together how a container can affect the way we feel and think. We have discussed some ways of looking at this phenomenon in this chapter. In the following chapter we discuss some of our experiences, cite some of the more interesting cases, include a number of reports we have received from others, and along the way offer some additional speculations about the nature of what is happening.

10

The Healing Phenomenon—II

"Phenomena is occurring in healing for which we have no diagnosis—no way of describing it—phenomena we must understand if medicine is going to meet the demands being made of it today."

With these words, Dr. Roy Menninger opened the proceedings of the First National Congress on Integrative Health, mentioned in the previous chapter. He found himself in agreement with the new movement in medicine today known as the holistic approach—medicine of the whole person—which conceives of health as a balanced state of man's total being, physical, chemical, electrical, emotional, mental, and spiritual.

Because science has now accepted the existence of the many dimensions of man, thanks primarily to the development of instruments capable of demonstrating their existence, other than traditional approaches to diagnosis and treatment have become viable. For reasons not entirely known, but probably in part due to its wider acknowledgment, all manner of nontraditional methods of diagnosis and healing has been brought to our attention. Perhaps one of the reasons for this growing phenomenon is that once a working hypothesis has been established the research, the testing, the introduction of technology and instruments can start; new discoveries then unfold somewhat rapidly. This development then involves persons of various disciplines in the effort, their skills are required, and a scientific field, such as medicine in this case, then becomes multidisciplinary. Instead of physicians only talking to physicians they have to fraternize with physicists, engineers, biologists, chemists, mathematicians, and so on. And when it is learned that the practitioners of other methods of healing have something going for them, that it can be scientifically demonstrated as valid, then suddenly showing up at gatherings are theologians; psychic, faith, and spiritual healers; shamans, yogis, clairvoyants, and medicine men. We have attended no less than five national medical meetings during the past three years when all of the above practitioners were in attendance.

Whereas a few years back the discussions at medical conferences were limited to such topics as organs, tissues, cells, and so on, the talk today includes electrical flow, energy force fields, intuitive components of the mind, spiritual aspects, and so forth. A person such as healer Dr. Olga Worrall can attend and make the following statement and it becomes as acceptable as if she had addressed herself to adrenal flow:

"Every healing physician and every unconventional healer works to this same goal. Their efforts, if correctly applied, are compatible and complementary. As to the actual source of the healing power, we can only say at this time that there is a 'something' out of which comes everything. Within this certain 'something' exists, among other things, Supreme Intelligence, Omnipotent Will and Immutable Law. This certain 'something' is neither energy nor matter but is the source of both. It has neither magnitude nor dimension. It is both timeless and spaceless. This

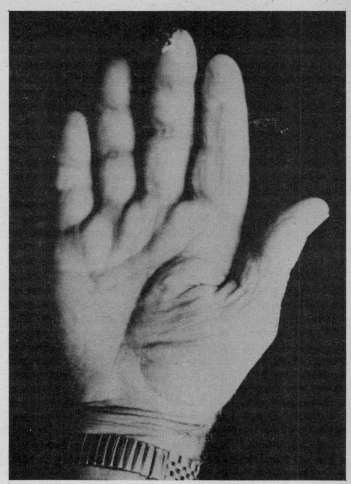

Ed Pettit's hand 6 weeks after accident.

is the source of the healing power which flows strictly in accordance with Immutable Law. The majority of people call this source 'God.' "

So it is within a new climate of medicine, a new way of looking at man and his universe, that we can talk about pyramids and the process of healing . . . not with tongue in cheek, not even with a note of apology. The idea that the shape of the space in which we might expose a part or all of ourselves shows as much evidence of fitting into the scientific domain as does the fact that the shape of an instrument affects its tone in the musical arena.

With as much legitimacy as we might list case histories in a medical report, we can direct our attention to the reports we have received from persons who have experienced some aspect of healing through the use of pyramids. It is through such information that we can gain greater insights into pyramid phenomena.

One of the most interesting cases of healing happened to one of us, Ed Pettit. The healing phenomena was so unusual that the well-known physician on the case gave us permission to use his name, provided us with x-rays, and had the attending hospital release its report in order that we might use it in the book.

I had completed the 16-by-16-foot base to an outside wooden pyramid and was sawing the interior wood when my right hand slipped into the blade of the circular saw. My wife rushed me to the hospital emergency section. The attending physician inspected the hand and stated that due to the extent of the injuries I would need the services of a reconstructive plastic surgeon "to put the hand back together."

Two and a half hours later Dr. W. E. Dalton arrived and I was taken into surgery. Afterward I was told that the two end joints of the two middle fingers would likely have to be removed, as the blood vessels supplying the ends of the fingers with blood would not be able to perform the task because they had been virtually destroyed.

The hospital "Operation Record" read:

"The patient caught his finger in a saw. He had multiple

fractures and multiple lacerations. He was given tetanus toxoid, antibiotics and had vigorously prep with Betadine prep and Betadine scrub solution after satisfactory digital block. The patient had 2 minor lacerations. One of the little finger and the other of the index finger. The index finger was somewhat stellate in character. It was debrided sharply and closed with interrupted 5/0 prolene. The little finger lacerations on the distal phalanx was 1 cm. in total length. This was simply closed after debridement of the skin edges. The most severe laceration and injury was in the long finger. He had two lacerations of the long finger. One was a 3 cm. flap laceration based on the radial digital artery and going across the entire tip of the finger to the ulna lateral surface. This was a 3 cm. in length and was roughly flap laceration with 1½ cm. based flap. This was debrided. It was sutured in place with interrupted prolene. In addition he had a 2½ cm. laceration of the middle finger at the junction of the middle and distal phalanges. This on the volar surface was similarly debrided and bleeding vessels were ligated. The wound was then closed with interrupted 5/0 prolene. The patient had a 3 cm. laceration of the ring finger extending from the dorsal side on the other. Fortunately the neurovascular bundles were not involved. After satisfactory debridement and irrigation this wound was similarly closed with 5/0 prolene. There were multiple fractures of the distal phalanges of the ring and long finger. These were fixed with Riordan and the wounds were then cleansed and were dressed with multiple dressings and a bulky hand dressing with volar splint. The patient was given instructions in elevation, given pain medications, antibiotics and an appointment for followup in my office."

X-rays showed that the phalanges, the end bones of the two fingers, were shattered as were the tendons, which would likely prevent movements of either of the two ends even if they were saved.

For the next two nights I sat with my hand inside a cardboard pyramid for one hour each night and then I made a return call to the doctor's office in order to see if infection was involved. At that time it was found that the end of the middle finger was coal black, indicating that no blood was being supplied to it. I was advised that the end of the finger, from the joint on, would probably have to be removed. The other finger seemed to be satisfactory, as far as blood supply was concerned. I continued to treat my hand in the pyramid.

Five days later I returned to the office fully expecting to return home minus the end of the finger. When the finger was unwrapped it was found, much to everyone's surprise, that the formerly black end had turned a healthy pink, with the exception of a small portion which remained black. Obviously, the end of the finger would not have to be removed, but it was thought that perhaps a skin graft would be needed to cover the black portion. One week later it was determined that a skin graft was not needed as it appeared that the black portion was covering tissue that might fill in the damaged area.

On November 2, 1975, I returned to the doctor's office and he made arrangements for me to have another set of x-rays taken for my own use. The x-rays showed that the bones had regrown, as indicated by the doctor's report. At this writing, seven weeks after the injury, I can move the ends of both the middle fingers and it appears that I will regain full use of the entire hand, something the doctor did not believe would happen.

I have kept the hand intermittently in a pyramid since the accident happened and I attribute the healing and regrowth of the bones and tissues, the tendons and blood vessels not only to the ability of a skilled surgeon but also to the healing powers of the pyramid.

I have also experienced a fringe benefit from using the pyramid. The little finger on the same hand was injured several years ago and I never regained feeling in it. Now it is almost back to normal feeling again; I can sense hot and cold and pressure. I had been forced to discontinue use of the finger for many things but now I am starting to use it again.

On November 6, 1975, Dr. W. Edward Dalton provided us with the following letter:

"I was asked to see Mr. Pettit on the 9th of September, 1975, to treat saw injuries to his index, long, ring, and little fingers on his right hand with multiple lacerations and fractures of the distal phalanges of the ring and long fingers. At surgery he had debridement and primary closure of multiple lacerations of all fingers. He had internal fixation of the fractures of the ring and long fingers. There was rather marked preoperative displacement of these fractures. Postoperatively he has done very well. His course has been rather remarkable in the lack of complications. He has a small eschar on the long finger, which is a result of poor circulation to a distally based flap at the time of the initial surgery. However, this is healing quite nicely. The amount of swelling is remarkably little.

"At this time, nearly two months after the surgery, he is having a reasonable amount of motion of both the proximal and distal interphalangeal joints of the injured fingers. I expect that we will see continued improvement in what seems to be a rather accelerated manner."

Following are reports of others who have had similar healing experiences:

"Pulled muscle crick in neck and shoulder. Sat in the pyramid for about 15 minutes and later for 30 minutes that same day. Helped loosen tightness and finally cleared the next day."

"For several years I have suffered back pain from accidental injuries, aggravated no doubt by stress and strain. I cannot really remember how long it has been since I had any freedom from this pain. On the evening of October 20th I spent about 40 minutes in Mr. Pettit's pyramid and had immediate relief from pain, felt completely relaxed, and had the best night's sleep in a long time. I am still free of pain today and am so grateful." This letter was from Jo Novak of Oklahoma City.

After approximately thirty minutes in our large outside pyramid Leonard Anthony wrote us the following note: "Felt easing or actually cessation of low back pain—

couldn't determine if it was my posture in the chair or the atmosphere—but the pain was gone.

"Dizzy upon arising but had indulged in much deep breathing in the pyramid and extremely short-breathed upon coming into open air. Feeling of short breath still with me half-hour later."

"Lower difficulties about one-fourth of what it was initially."

Tom Garrett told us of his experience with a broken toe:

"I was involved in a home accident that resulted in a broken little toe. The toe had been jammed into the leg of a chair and was pushed so far as to form a right-angle to the side of my foot. I could hear a distinct 'snap' as the toe was broken. Swelling was immediate, and I headed for my six-foot pyramid in the hope of some much needed relief from the pain that seemed to double in intensity with each throb. After about fifteen or twenty minutes I noticed an increase in pain and a more distinctive throbbing sensation. This continued for about ten minutes, then the pain seemed to decrease as it throbbed with each heartbeat. When the pain had stopped, I remained in the pyramid for another two hours and took a nap. When I awoke, the pain was still gone and the swelling had decreased noticeably. I extended my treatment another hour that evening before going to bed. The next morning, little swelling remained and I was able to walk normally with very little discomfort."

Jan Norriss of Tucson read our book *The Secret Power of Pyramids,* immediately constructed one, and started her research. "The pyramid has given me a new lease on life —it's such a challenge," Edith Sayre Armstrong, writing in the December 4, 1975, issue of *The Arizona Daily Star,* quoted Norriss as saying: "The pyramid is amazing. After putting my face cream inside, I used it on one side of my face and it lifted my face and erased the wrinkles." The Armstrong article continues: "Now don't get too excited about this . . . but I placed a roll of foil in the pyramid and gave a piece to a friend of mine who has had hip and knee pains for years. He taped the foil to his hip and knee and after an hour and a half, the pain was gone for the first time in years. You better take that with a grain of salt, though, because I don't know the long-range effect."

Mary had developed a small sore on the inner lining of her mouth. It had caused her a great deal of discomfort for three or four days. She rinsed her mouth with water that had been treated for thirty days in a six-foot pyramid. She rinsed before retiring and noticed a distinct throbbing and intensified pain in the area around the sore. All through the following day she was aware of this throbbing. The pain subsided in the latter part of the day and was totally gone the next morning. The sore had also disappeared.

Leah Ingram of Oklahoma City wrote us:

"I fell September 4th and broke the small bone in my left leg. I hope the doctor will let me have the x-rays so I can send them to you. [The doctor did provide her with the x-rays.] I am 52 years old and never had a broken bone except my arm in the first grade. My doctor said because of my age it would take at least eight weeks for it to mend and maybe more. Dave built me a small pyramid to sit on the bed so I could put my leg in it. We found, however, that I would have to put both legs in the pyramid in order to lie down. He cut a cross in the pyramid and I put both legs in with the injured leg propped on a pillow to raise it and help with the weight of the cast.

"My leg did not hurt me from that time on and did not hardly swell. After I had been up during the day my leg would be somewhat tight in the cast but it would be fine again the next morning. I told my doctor at the end of two weeks that my leg was not hurting and that I would like to x-ray it again as I was sure it was all right. He said no, that children didn't even heal that quick. I didn't go back to the doctor the next week because I was so far behind at home I stayed home and straightened up the house. My leg still didn't bother me, just the weight of the cast.

"When I went back to the doctor on October 13th I

asked him to x-ray my leg. There was no sign on the second x-ray to show where my leg was broken. He laid the first x-ray over the second one to check the area that had been broken just to make sure he hadn't overlooked anything. He said I must really be a healthy person and in good shape. I told him I had been climbing the stairs at home since the second week and that I had not missed one day's work since I broke my leg. He thought it was remarkable especially since I had had no pain at all during this time."

Quite a few reports mention the easing and elimination of headaches, also the loss of tension.

"Extremely bad headache. I sat in my pyramid for approximately twenty minutes and my head improved considerably. Still a touch of a headache but not nearly so severe."

"After sitting in a pyramid for a while I felt very sleepy, relaxed and my sinuses had cleared."

"After completing my six-foot pyramid, my leg and back muscles were extremely sore. After leaning the four sides together, I sat in it for several minutes and noticed a return of my energy. I felt so much better that I didn't notice the lack of soreness in my muscles until later in the evening."

Joe Wall, Milwaukee, told us, "You probably remember my friend that had a very bad case of psoriasis on her right hand and on the back of her neck. Her time in the pyramid, along with deep concentration, prayer, and belief in the Infinite help has cured the psoriasis on her hand. She has a faint red area on her neck, but that is also disappearing. Also, for the last month, she has had a great deal of sinus drainage into her throat resulting in a bad cough and gagging. She started spending one hour a day in the pyramid and now the problem is completely cleared up. These are facts!"

Wall also stated that the pyramid had been of help to his mother: "We have had my mother spend some time in the pyramid. She states that her nerves are calmer and that she has a distinct feeling of well being after leaving the pyramid."

Tom Garrett wrote us about a friend who used his pyramid to get rid of a headache:

"Subject had headache from staring into the sun all afternoon at a college football game. When he left the pyramid, he stated that he had noticed nothing unusual while inside, outside of the fact that he had been distracted by children running around in front of the house. This was odd because the children he was referring to were about a half block away. His sense of hearing seemed to be stimulated. He commented that his headache had gone away but hadn't noticed it until he had been out of the pyramid for several minutes. He was very surprised, and being one of the most skeptical people I have ever known, his response was of great interest to me."

Garrett also wrote, "This subject was complaining of sinus congestion. She sat in the pyramid and returned to the living room to report that her breathing was much freer and easier."

Feelings of renewed energy and the loss of fatigue from sitting, sleeping, or meditating in pyramids are frequently reported and this may be due to electromagnetic stimulation. In an article, "Medical Applications of Magnetism," in the October 1972 issue of *Bulletin of the Atomic Scientists,* Dr. E. H. Frei states, "Muscle stimulation is an area where some research has recently been conducted, and results show that practically all muscles will contract as the magnetic field on them is altered. It is widely assumed that the stimulation is of an electrical nature caused by electromagnetic induction. An electric field produced by a changing magnetic field can send a current through a cell and in this way stimulate all kinds of muscles."

In the same article, Dr. Frei quotes from the patent awarded in 1922 to S. Maeshima of Tokyo: ". . . For transmitting magnetism into the human body, which, giving a slight stimulus to the nerve periphery and tissue cells, accelerates blood circulation and skin excretion and regulates the metabolism, thereby promoting health and keeping off diseases or assisting recovery therefrom."

In *Consciousness, Energy and Substance in Christian Healing* Dr. Griffith Evans states, "If all forms of action are mediated by electromagnetic radiation, then all chemical actions, all metabolic exchanges, all nerve impulses, and thought itself, are, to say the least, accompanied by electric changes. Ever since Max Planck, these changes are known to be exchanges of definite amounts of energy between systems in mutal resonance, and since the concept of energy exchange is impossible without the symbol of the wave-cycle (Schrödinger), it must follow that the configurations of the respective systems are geometrical, interlocking and measurable."

Following are some of the comments we have received regarding rest and renewal of energy:

"Have had insomnia for several years and took several sleeping pills every night. I tried sleeping in a pyramid. The first night I took three pills; the second night two pills; the third night I took one pill. After that I discontinued the pills. It has been two weeks and I feel like a million dollars in the morning. No more pills for me."

"I wrapped pyramid-treated foil inside my night cap. Have had trouble concentrating but it is much better now, and I don't get headaches when I read late."

"After about twenty minutes inside the pyramid it seems as if your body has a fresh charge of oxygen and energy. When falling asleep, the sleep is deep. None of our family has spent more than an hour inside the pyramid. The feeling of having been asleep seems to stay with you for quite a while."

"I was so chronically fatigued that my doctor started giving me strong vitamin B-12 shots to pep me up. After starting to sleep in the pyramid I have found that I can get along without the shots."

Florence McClure is a graduate registered nurse who has been in continuous practice since 1925. She became interested in pyramids and had a seven-foot-tall pyramid made of green translucent rigid plastic constructed in her backyard. Following is our brief interview with her about healing experiences:

"What were you saying about your hand?"

"My hands have been paining me all of the time. After using my pyramid for about twenty minutes a day for two days I experienced relief. Then I was in the pyramid for two and a half hours and have not had pain since that time. The pain is completely gone. I also had a bladder infection that completely cleared in two twenty-minute sessions. And the tension is gone from my shoulders—I have no aches, no pains, no headaches."

"You went into training as a nurse when?"

"Oh, I went into training in 1925 and I've practiced all these years."

"You mentioned something earlier about a friend?"

"Oh, this friend of mine is eighty-three years old. She came to see me about sitting in my pyramid. She had been having trouble with her blood pressure. She spent thirty minutes inside the pyramid and her blood pressure stabilized. She said she felt such peace and quiet. She felt fine and was pretty thrilled about it."

"You also mentioned something about your daughter?"

"My daughter hurt her back. She was in intense pain. She started spending about twenty to thirty minutes in the pyramid each day and her pain is all gone now. I agree with you on what you said about doctors. No one should forgo medical attention and they should follow the doctor's orders strictly; they should never have so much faith in anything that they would dismiss their doctors, but I believe that the pyramid shape can be a great supplement. It is surprising, they all come out of the pyramid and say the same thing. 'Oh, I feel so good . . . I have more energy . . . the aches and pains are gone.' I know how I felt. I was so tense. It may have been the pain in my hands, but it's funny, it was throbbing like a toothache in both hands . . . you know, you want to go around with both hands in the air. It was miraculous, actually, you know, you are not conscious of anything, you just don't hurt anymore."

A discussion of pyramids and healing would not be complete without telling about Thomas Thompson of Vancouver, Canada, a remarkable man who for fifty years has dedicated himself to the healing and helping of others. His ability to heal has brought him a long line of followers. In his half-century of healing he has tried many methods but is quick to point out that "it is usually the seeker and the administrator getting together that actually produces the results. Understanding of the approach and the acceptance of methods of healing are important to receive a definite healing, whether it is from a doctor, the physicians, the minister or any of the different methods of healing that are currently offered," he said, and adds, "In actuality, the patients themselves are the final proof. Too often, the seeker does not realize that there is a power which can bring about the desired results."

Thompson has used both pyramids and cones for many years in his healing work. In some instances he found that the cones worked better than the pyramids. We asked him to relate some of his healing experiences with both pyramids and cones. He was kind enough to allow us to use the following experiences in this chapter on healing. The cases are more interesting when told in his words. The first case has to do with a type of iron-lung apparatus with pyramids placed on top of the box:

"The box was shaped like an iron lung with the head sticking out. Three pyramids were placed on top of the lid. Everyone using this box reported that all tension seemed to drain out of them in two or three minutes. They became so relaxed that invariably they would doze off to sleep. I usually woke them in twenty minutes to half an hour.

"One old gentleman used to come down every Saturday morning. He managed one of the hotels downtown and would be very hypertensive with all the things which happened in the hotel. He would stay there for an hour and come out young and vibrant again, ready for another week's work. He was only eighty-three years of age.

"Many used the box and found relief of a variety of

symptoms that they couldn't seem to get rid of in any other way. The pyramids seemed to give them a new life and energy. Their minds seemed to clear of many difficulties. The healings with the pyramids and the cones took on a more definite effect when they were built to correspond with the need of the person requesting help. I incorporated the feeling of the individual into the cone or pyramid. Between the cones and the pyramids, the cones were the more flexible of the two to work with.

"I have found that the cone and the pyramid, used in many different ways, i.e., placed on the head, or the feet, or the abdomen, or wherever the person is experiencing pain, soon relieves the pain.

"A friend of mine who had helped me demonstrate the cones many times tried to get his wife to try one for her bleeding hemorrhoids. She had suffered with them for years. They had become so bad that the doctor had prescribed surgery. My friend took a cone home but his wife tossed it in a corner because she thought it was dangerous and would have nothing to do with it. She could not throw it out because her husband would become angry. She was cleaning one day and sat down to rest. She had a funny sensation around the hemorrhoids, but when she got up to check out what was going on, the itching stopped, so she sat down again to drink her tea. When she sat down again, it started all over. Strangely, every time she got up the itching stopped and when she sat down it started again. Bewildered, she looked around and found that the cone had gotten under her chair. The next day she deliberately sat on the chair with the cone under it.

"She had an appointment with her doctor to decide whether it would be one or two weeks before the appointed surgery. The examination revealed that the hemorrhoids had shrunk and there was no need for surgery at that time. She was told to come back in a week to be checked. Every morning for that week, she sat on the chair with the cone under it. When she went to the doctor again, she knew what he was going to say because she felt so different. She felt like her whole body had changed. The doctor confirmed her feelings. She would not be having the operation.

"Another victory for the pyramid was a lady who had suffered for years with a problem of an abnormal tongue. Her taste, speech, and food consumption were affected, in addition to which she suffered from an extremely sore throat and her tongue was swollen and a very dark brown. She was afraid that she might be wasting my time, but we tried the pyramid over her throat as she lay down on the davenport. The pyramid was placed so the point was directly over her throat.

"She was to use the pyramid for half an hour a day and phone me when there was any change. In two days, she called and the soreness had disappeared and the color was starting to change from the root of the tongue, the tip still being dark brown. She was instructed to keep up the treatments. The next day she called and asked me to come to see her. When I arrived, she stuck out her tongue at me. She was so excited. The tongue had resumed its normal size and color and she could taste food again. As an added bonus, her eyesight had improved.

"The cone and pyramid took a definite part in the restoration and confidence of a young lady who was the owner of a beauty parlor in downtown Vancouver. She explained that her beauty parlor meant so much to her as she had invested $25,000 and three years of hard work. She told me of a peculiar accident that she had had a week previous.

"She had forgotten something in her house and had jumped out of her car, forgetting to put on the brake. In front of her house were two large pillars of cement which held up the walkway. She tried pushing against the car to stop it but a slight incline got the best of her and she was driven against the pillars. Her arm was smashed against the column of cement; the bone, wrist to the elbow, was shattered. Someone rushed her to the doctor, but she was told that it was going to be about a year before she would be able to use the arm and hand. He put on a very heavy cast, saying that it was necessary that the cast go up to the shoulder to hold the elbow in a definite place. But he said that the difficulty was that the bone in the elbow was so shattered that they might have to take the cast off and operate to take out the little splinters of bone. He told her this so that she would not expect a quick recovery.

"She began to realize what had happened and viewed her three years of hard work going down the drain. She sensed that the beauty parlor girls would go into business for themselves and she would be ruined. A mutual friend had told her to come and see me, that I could help her.

"After a lengthy conversation, I persuaded her that I would do my best. But, I wouldn't guarantee her recovery until she could specify a definite date by which she would work toward being well. She indicated six weeks to six months as the time she had in mind. Six weeks being her preference, but six months seeming the most realistic. She was extremely concerned that I be totally honest about the length of time my treatment would cover and that I not give her any time limits that could not be met.

"I told her that in six weeks she would be back to the beauty parlor. That in itself seemed to give her hope instead of that downcast feeling she entered my office with. She said that she would go along with this time schedule. At this I told her that there were two things that she had to do: (1) Use the pyramid and (2) use the cone. I added that if she used these as I told her, she would be surprised at what would happen. She asked, 'Aren't you going to pray, aren't you going to do something else besides just using those?' I told her, 'No, you'll have to do your own praying.' I was just offering the pyramids and cones.

"A week later she returned; the pain had gone the first night. There was no more pain in her elbow or her hand. The second week she phoned to say that she was beginning to feel life in the hand and by the third week the doctor wanted to change the cast as the swelling had gone down so much.

"The break down the arm seemed to knit, the splinters seemed to disappear, and the elbow was free. By the fourth week she was washing hair in the beauty parlor and during the fifth week she was once again setting hair. At six weeks, her shoulder, hand, elbow, wrist—everything—was in order and she was operating the beauty parlor again. After that she placed pyramids on the shelf above where her customers sat while waiting. She found that this was relaxing to them while they were waiting.

"I was called one morning by a very athletic young man who asked me if I could do anything for retarded children. He told me that he had thirty children from the ages of nine to sixteen. They were all retarded and he thought it would take two years before anything could be accomplished with them. He had heard about the cones and wondered if it was possible for the group to be helped collectively. I suggested to him that I come to his place to see just exactly in what way I might help. I brought thirty cones with me and suggested a large pyramid be put in the center of the room. The day I went down I was touched by the condition of the children. He told me that they were in his charge for two years. He had a contract that each one of them would be completely well in his findings or well enough to go home. He had a waiting list of 175 others, but he couldn't possibly take more than thirty with his present situation. As I went over the entire place with him, I saw that each room had the possibility for placement of a cone. He warned me not to make the cones easily taken down because some of his patients had a habit of destroying anything that was movable. So, I sealed down some cones and left the rest loose, suggesting that there might be times when he could put the cones over the feet or over the abdomen. To my surprise, within thirty days he contacted me and suggested that I come down as soon as possible. When I arrived, he said, 'Mr. Thompson, I don't know whether or not I should keep those cones.' I asked what had happened. He informed me that there had been so much improvement in that month that many of the parents wanted to take their children home immediately.

"The cones seemed to have made such a vast improvement that I wondered what would have happened if he had kept them. But he had lost so much control of the situation that he asked me to remove the cones.

"I have witnessed the effects of a pyramid on animals, especially horses. I have a friend who trains race horses, raises them, and boards sick horses. He asked if I thought the pyramids would be of benefit to the horses. I suggested that a pyramid be placed in each stall above the feeding pail. He had been trained to use the pendulum and this alone showed quite a difference after just one night. He found that he did not need to keep the sick horses more than two or three days whereas before it sometimes took weeks. While watching a horse work out one day, he told me that the horse had had trouble breathing. It could only work a short time before it was blowing. Now, as I could see, it was normal."

Pyramids appear to have been beneficial to our pets, particularly a large German shepherd. Whereas we have had experimental pyramids around for several years, he was not allowed inside them as experiments were always in process. But when we built the large outside pyramid, he was allowed to spend some time inside. This he was eager to do and did so at every opportunity. For more than a year he had been partially crippled with arthritis, but we started noticing an amazing difference in his mobility after allowing him in the pyramid. Now, for the first time in many months, he played catch, wanted to be chased, and so on.

A number of people have written to us about experiences with their pets and healing allegedly as a result of exposing them to pyramid space:

"Our dog Sham has always seemed to have asthma or a breathing problem, especially if she gets excited. We remembered tonight that this hasn't happened since she has been in the pyramid with our daughter."

Asthma was also mentioned by Florence McClure when we interviewed her: "My little Boston terrier has asthma and every day she would have attacks and was unable to get her breath. She hasn't had asthma trouble since she has been getting in the pyramid with me. And I have a toy poodle that has had chronic sore throats since she had her tonsils out. Since her exposure to the pyramid she has had no more throat problems; it's entirely cleared up."

"Our cocker spaniel is ten years old and has had bad rheumatism for several years. We built her a new doghouse in the shape of a pyramid. She is now starting to show some improvement."

"Our dog sleeps in the garage beside the pyramid and has grown the best looking and heaviest coat of hair that we have ever seen on her. She seems to be extremely healthy now and feels better than any time we can recall."

Several people have mentioned that they have obtained beneficial results by treating foil inside a pyramid and then placing it under their dog's bedding. One person put the treated foil in his bird cage and reported that his bird had stopped dropping feathers and was beginning to sing again.

Healing of animals as well as humans was mentioned by Dr. Olga Worrall in the talk mentioned earlier: "Over the years I have discovered that this healing force is not only effective in healing humans, but also dogs, cats, horses, birds, chickens, and even plants responded to this mysterious energy."

If the use of pyramids is beneficial to animals, as it appears to be, that should be welcome news to all animal lovers, ourselves included. But what was of particular interest to us in these reports was the evidence that we are dealing with something more than psychosomatic-type illnesses. If humans reported healing benefits and these successes could not be duplicated with animals, we would tend to suspect that the pyramid was nothing more than an effective placebo. This does not appear to be the case.

We have received many other reports that have not been mentioned simply because they warrant further investigation. Some of these have had to do with various serious illnesses such as cancer, tuberculosis, diabetes, and heart ailments. Due to the seriousness of these illnesses and the fact that we do not have documented information, they have not been discussed for fear of offering some people what might prove to be false hopes.

In the two chapters on healing we have related our own experiences and those of others, and we have endeavored to offer some explanations along the way. There is nothing sacred about our explanations . . . we are quite sure that at best they are only partial. But we have tried to supply scientific data where possible in the hopes that it would provide a framework for greater exploration.

11

Nutritional Alchemy

Pyramids will not change base metals into gold but they perform their own brand of alchemy with food commodities. Perhaps in a world justly concerned with growing enough food and the preserving of the food we do have without pollutants, the role of the pyramid will be more important than changing the structure of metal. Anyway, if we ever succeeded in making gold, it wouldn't be long before it would be worth no more than other metals. On the other hand, our need for food will continue to grow.

For more than three years we have been using pyramids to dehydrate various fruits and vegetables. Although the dehydration rate is not always the same, taking longer sometimes than other times, the food items do not spoil inside the pyramid. When completely dried, they can be stored for an indefinite period of time. Judging from the number of recent magazine articles and several books on how to dry and store fruits and vegetables, this method of preserving food is regaining a following. The pyramid serves as a simple and effective way of doing this. Meat also dehydrates very well inside pyramids. We have experienced no meat spoilage and have received no reports of spoilage from others using pyramids for this purpose.

Laboratory tests show that the growth of microorganisms is retarded or stopped completely inside pyramids and spoilage does not occur in the absence of bacteria. We have put dehydrated meat on shelves without refrigeration and have eaten it months later. It tastes as good as any dried beef or venison and even seems less tough. We have found that aluminum foil can be treated in a pyramid for several days and then be used as a substitute pyramid. It apparently absorbs the pyramid energy and can retain it for a number of days. Food items, including meat, wrapped in the treated foil can be preserved without refrigeration for some time. However, to determine the length of time, it is wise to do some experimenting with one's own pyramid, as there are a number of factors involved and the time may vary. We have found that foil absorbs an optimal charge in approximately fourteen days, and will retain it outside the pyramid for about the same length of time.

When we first tried storing food without refrigeration, we wondered if it wouldn't be attacked by insects. We were pleasantly surprised to learn that insects will enter the pyramid but will clear out very shortly thereafter. This also happens with food wrapped in treated foil; they will approach the package, perhaps even crawl momentarily on the outside, but then will leave. It may be that there is something about the frequency field or the resonating factor inside the pyramid that drives insects away. We have a friend who decided to test the insect repellent qualities of the pyramid with a bunch of ants. He gathered the ants from a hill in his garden and placed some of them inside a pyramid and another group outside the pyramid. Near each group he poured some sugared milk. The ants inside the pyramid approached the milk but soon retreated beyond the enclosure. They joined the ants outside hungrily swarming about the milk. Our plants inside pyramids have been bug-free, but we have noticed aphids on some of the control plants.

As regards the preservation of meat, the late Verne Cameron of Elsinore, California, mentioned elsewhere in this book for his research twenty years ago in unusual energy fields, experimented with the dehydration of pork, which spoils very quickly without refrigeration. He put a piece of fresh pork inside a pyramid kept in his bathroom. This was to be the acid test, for the bathroom was high in humidity, which normally would stimulate spoilage. Within ten days, Cameron reported the pork had mummified. He ate it six months later after it had remained in his bathroom pyramid for the entire duration. He stated that the meat was perfectly edible.

The pyramid also works its alchemy on the quality of foods, making them taste better and in some instances easier to digest. Experiments with measuring the differences in properties of food inside and outside pyramids are discussed in the final chapter. However, we have conducted a number of blind tests with subjects in which we have asked them to select food items or beverages that had been treated in the pyramid from the control item. In each case the experimental and control item were halves of the same food item, or from the same bottle, or whatever. Nine out of ten people selected the pyramid-treated food as having the best taste.

"There is a definite difference," a housewife known to friends and acquaintances as an excellent cook told us. "One doesn't have to be a gourmet to tell that the pyramid-treated food (she had been tested on salad dressing, cheddar cheese, and sirloin) is fresher and there is more depth or body to the taste."

Thinking that perhaps we were mentally projecting the correct selections to the subjects, we tried a double-blind test. We had a neighbor mark the food products in such a way that we would not know which was which until after the experiment. Eight out of nine test subjects still selected the pyramid-treated items.

We have been drinking pyramid water fairly regularly for a couple of years and are convinced that it has improved our digestion. One of us has very low hydrochloric-acid content. When pyramid water is taken with the meal, digestion seems to be markedly better. Several other persons have written us reporting much the same results.

Hydrochloric acid is an enzyme and this may be one of the clues as to why food tastes better, is more tender, and more easily digested after being treated in pyramids. It is known that enzymes have a bearing on the taste of foods. Meat prepared with enzyme compounds before cooking is more tender, and of course, in the body enzymes break down food before it can be digested. As the evidence seems to indicate the presence of increased magnetic fields within pyramid space, it may be that the enriched magnetic field affects the growth activity of enzymes.

The effect of magnetic fields on enzymes has been extensively explored by Sister Justa Smith, Ph.D., chairman of the Natural Sciences Concentration at Rosary Hill College in Buffalo and director of research for the Human Dimensions Institute.

As a biochemist, Dr. Smith maintains that the proper functioning of the body is directly related to the proper balance of all the enzyme systems in the body. Healing and the maintenance of good health, according to Dr. Smith, relates to the metabolic reactions of each cell catalyzed by an enzyme. If enzymes play this important role in health maintenance, as Dr. Smith insists, and enzymes can be affected by magnetic fields, then it seems reasonable to hypothesize that the magnetic fields generated or enhanced inside pyramids are at least partly responsible for the variety of healing experiences reported for the use of pyramids in treatment. This subject is explored further in the chapters on "The Healing Phenomenon."

In his experiments with Dr. Smith, Oskar Estebany treated each time two vials of enzymes in water solution. One sample was normal and the other had been damaged by ultraviolet light. A third sample was treated with a magnetic field of 13,000 gauss.

As to the manner in which the solution was assayed, Dr. Smith told the conference, "The activity was measured on a chromogenic substrate; the substrate is that material on which the enzyme acts. I insist upon the word 'chromogenic' in there, because, as I said originally, this whole solution looks like water, but as the enzyme acts upon the substrate it cleaves off a molecule that is colored. Therefore, it is very simple to put the reaction mixture into a spectrophotometer and simply measure the rate at which color was added to the solution."

When the solutions were examined, it was found that Estebany had to some extent "healed" the damaged enzymes and he had increased the activity of the healthy enzymes close to the same degree as had the magnetic field applied to the third vial.

Another parallel can be drawn between the effects of pyramids on enzymes and that of a magnetic force field. We have treated plants with force fields created by a multiwave oscillator, a device that allegedly raises the vibratory rate of cells, tissues, and so on by multiwave stimulation. The growth rate of these plants closely resembled those inside pyramids. We assumed, therefore, that the pyramid and multiwave oscillator shared some common force fields. A friend of ours who has an extremely low amount of hydrochloric acid in his system and has a difficult time maintaining his weight because of the lack of digestive juices, started using a multiwave oscillator for treatment. In a very short time he had gained needed weight, the first in a long time, presumedly due to the increased enzyme activity stimulated by the magnetic force fields. We wondered, then, if persons using pyramids would also experience this seeming balancing of enzymes in their bodies. Our question appeared to be partially answered at least when we heard from several overweight correspondents that they had lost weight after starting to meditate in pyramids. And shortly after this we received reports that persons with underweight problems had gained weight via the same approach. We do not wish to infer that the overweight and the underweight will find the perfect environment inside pyramids. There are likely many variables involved, some of which may be psychosomatic or simply a matter of positive thinking. However, the evidence thus far would seem to warrant further investigation.

According to the laws of chemistry that held forth for more than one and a half centuries, elements can be shifted about in different combinations but cannot be transmuted one to another: A and B can become AB, but A cannot become B.

The first negation of this law occurred shortly after the turn of the century with the discovery of radioactivity, which revealed that about twenty elements could change into something else. With the development of nuclear physics, certain elements were created which were believed to have long vanished or never existed in their natural state.

Nevertheless, chemists still contend that it is impossible to create another element by chemical reaction. This concept is now being contested by French scientist, biologist Louis Kervran. Contending that biological transmutation is factual, Kervran cites chickens as an example of his theory. Hens need calcium to form the shells of their eggs, but in one experiment they were fed no calcium. Their diet included, instead, mica, which is a silicate of aluminum and potash, and the hens produced the required calcium themselves. Thus it would seem that potassium together with an ion of hydrogen was transmuted to give calcium.

Kervran points out that when chickens hatch they contain four times more lime than was originally present in the egg, that cress weeds grown under a glass bell in nothing but distilled water produce sprouts with twice the sulfur in the seeds, that algae produce iodine, and so on. In a recent book, *Biological Transmutations,* Kervran states that his purpose is "to show that matter has a property heretofore unseen, a property which is neither present in chemistry nor in nuclear physics in its present state."

Pursuing Kervran's ideas, Dr. Rudolf Hauschka contends that life cannot possibly be interpreted in chemical terms as life is not the result of the combination of elements but something preceding the elements. "Is it not more reasonable," he asks in the book *The Nature of Substance*, "to suppose that life existed long before matter and was the product of a pre-existent spiritual cosmos?"

This concept relates closely to the models of life discussed in the chapter "The Serpent's Fire." In this earlier material we described physical materialization as the final step in the process of universal energy moving through what we called the seven principles of man: those being spirit, soul, higher mind (intuitive), lower mind (rational), astral (emotional), etheric, and physical. This model is compatible with the idea that physical forms can be more accurately viewed as energy fields and that both, upon closer observation, are revealed as mental structures. In this view, consciousness is the basic substance of the universe.

We also described the progression of life from the mineral stages, to plants, to animals and man, according to Tibetan mysticism and, according to some scholars, the ancient Egyptian mystery schools. This model considers all life forms evolving toward spirit. In other words, everything is in the process of becoming something else whether we are speaking of subnuclear particles, human beings, or planets. Within the mystical tradition, transmutation is a requirement for life to exist. A must become B, whether the item in question is organic or inorganic. Everything from particles to universes is dynamic and not static. The only stable component, according to this tradition, is Universal Mind. Only this view can no longer be considered as just the mystical one—it is quickly becoming the basis for the new physics.

If the ancient builders of the Great Pyramid conceived of the concept of transmutation, we wonder if they would have not incorporated these principles into their construction. Was one of the purposes of the Great Pyramid to serve as a kind of master alchemist? While we do not find it and its modern-day progenies changing lead to gold, we do find them adding an unknown ingredient that seems to work toward raising both object—food, water, razor blades—and subject—humans—toward their optimal state. Upon drinking pyramid water one wonders if this isn't what water was supposed to be and upon tasting food treated in a pyramid the question again follows. Experiencing the elevating influence of forces within the pyramid, the meditator can't help but feel himself raised to higher levels of being. This would seem to be alchemy at its best.

On a wind-eroded cove of gorse and sand in a remote corner of northern Scotland exists the new Garden of Eden. A few years ago this patch of derelict soil—just beyond the heath where the three witches told Macbeth he would be Thane of Glamis and Cawdor—was the unsightly encampment of tin cans and rundown mobile homes.

Outside of the broom and quitch grass, gorse bushes, and long-suffering firs, nothing else grew and no one believed it would ever be otherwise . . . no one, that is except an ex-RAF squadron leader and two clairvoyants. Today it is a paradise of lush vegetation. Thousands from all over the world have gone there, including eminent scientists. The miracle of Findhorn has become a living legend.

What is so important about Findhorn and the people who founded it concerns a new way of looking at forces in the universe. It is a nice story to tell about people with faith who carried out the impossible dream; their garden grew and they lived happily ever after. But the real message in the rose bushes and tea leaves is that forces apparently do exist that can set aside or overcome conditions that we have considered omnipotent. According to established rules, the only factors involved in the growing of plants are the climate, amount of moisture, contents of the soil, and proper care and cultivation of the plants.

But Peter Caddy, his wife, Eileen, and Dorothy McLean had none of these ingredients working for them, except for the caring factor. In the end it was the only one that really mattered. Trees grew, flowers bloomed profusely, vegetables grew to record size, and the only addition to the soil that the agriculture experts could find was a thin layer of compost. It can't be happening, they said, but it was and crowds from everywhere were the witnesses.

A United Nations agriculture expert and professor of agriculture at several universities, Professor R. Lindsay Robb, visited Findhorn just before Christmas and went on record: "The vigor, health and bloom of the plants in the garden at midwinter on land which is almost barren powdery sand cannot be explained by the moderate dressings of compost, nor indeed by the application of any known cultural methods of organic husbandry. There are other factors and they are vital ones."

It is these unknown "vital factors" that are of interest to us here. The Caddys and Dorothy McLean finally admitted that their X-factor had nothing to do with secret fertilizer formulas. They proceeded according to information they received through their clairvoyant powers and this knowledge probed behind the secondary physical factors involved in plant growth.

The group told reporters that the most important contribution man can make to plant growth is the radiation he puts into the soil while cultivating it. Dorothy McLean said she came to realize that plants are constantly affected by radiation from the earth and the cosmos. She said these radiations were more important than chemical elements or microbiotic organisms, and that these radiations were subject fundamentally to the mind of man.

Commenting on the Findhorn phenomena, Peter Tompkins and Christopher Bird stated in *The Secret Life of Plants,* "Parting the veil into other worlds and other vibrations beyond the limits of the electromagnetic spectrum may well go a long way to explain the mysteries which are incomprehensible to physicists who limit their looking

Milk sample above apex of 6-foot pyramid in shop.

to what they can see with their physical eyes and their instruments."

When the soil in Caddy's garden was analyzed it was discovered that there were no deficiencies—surprising since the soil in the area was depleted of almost everything. Analysis of the compost added to the soil failed to reveal a reason for the difference. The soil came up with minerals that were not there before and that were not added from any physical source.

In our pyramid research we have found that plants grow faster inside than outside pyramids. The experimental plants are grown in the same soil and with the same amount of water and light as the control plants. We have grown plants inside containers made of the same materials and of the same volume as pyramid enclosures and the results are not the same. Some X-factor contributes to the growth of the plant in the pyramid.

In *The Secret Power of Pyramids* we described our work with time-lapse photography in which we observed the movement of plants inside and outside pyramids. The experimental plants made pronounced gyrations whereas the control plants hardly moved.

Milk oftentimes changes to yogurt inside the pyramid and recently several articles have appeared in national magazines proclaiming that yogurt is better for human consumption than milk; it contains more enzymes and is easier to digest. Once again, the pyramid appears to influence items to transmute to a higher level of being.

"Although the white man may use all of his knowledge —his chemistry, his biology, botany, engineering, and so on—he will not be able to return the soil, the water, and the air to its original purity," Rolling Thunder, chief medicine man of the Shoshone Indian Nation, told us at a gathering of scientists sponsored by the Menninger Foundation several years ago. "You have technical knowledge but you are unaware of vital forces that are not physical and they are the ones that truly count. Without this knowledge, you cannot penetrate the secrets of nature. It takes greater wisdom than chemistry to turn water into wine . . ."

12

A Special Place

The sorcerer Don Juan tells Carlos Castaneda that there is a special spot and that he must find it. This place is on the porch of the house and it is different, for if he finds it—and this he must do alone—he will experience peace and strength and happiness. Carlos Castaneda sits, he lies down, he even rolls around on the floor, but nothing happens. Then he chances to focus his eyes on a spot directly in front of him: the entire world turns greenish yellow. And then "suddenly, at a point near the middle of the floor, I became aware of another change of hue," he explains in *The Teachings of Don Juan*. "At a place to my right, still in the periphery of my field of vision, the greenish yellow became intensely purple. I concentrated my attention on it. The purple faded into a pale, but still brilliant, color which remained steady for the time I kept my attention on it." He tried lying down on this spot, but "I felt an unusual apprehension. It was more like a physical sensation of something pushing on my stomach. I jumped up and retreated in one movement. The hair on my neck pricked up. My legs had arched slightly, my trunk was bent forward, and my arms stuck out in front of me rigidly with my fingers contracted like a claw. I walked back involuntarily and . . . slumped to the floor." Castaneda had found his spot.

"For many years I have had a favorite spot in a wooded area on our place. I think maybe it found me rather than my finding it," the attractive young housewife told us. "I go there to meditate even when the weather isn't too pleasant and I always feel protected. But I'm telling you this because the very first time that I went inside a pyramid I was overwhelmed by the feeling of being in another very special place. With my eyes closed, I could easily imagine I was back at my wooded spot."

"Don't arbitrarily pick a spot in which to meditate just because it looks comfortable or secluded," our meditation teacher told us. "Don't be in a hurry, take your time, but once you find it, always go there whenever you can, alone, and try to protect this place from any other use."

In her books, Alice A. Bailey described special places on earth that were meant to be used for certain purposes, such as worship, meditation, healing, and so on. These places were the result, she said, of a grand design of energy fields encircling the earth. Where they crossed, energy grids were formed and vortices having special energy forces.

The ancients allegedly were aware of these energy paths, and where they crossed became the site of a temple, school, or other structure. According to this theory, pyramids were located on the vortices and the Great Pyramid became the hub of all this activity. Whether true or not, models designed according to the specifications of the Great Pyramid seem to create within their space a field different in property from other space in the environment. Perhaps pyramids create their own special place, or perhaps the special energy forces flowing about the earth are attracted by pyramids.

Of the energy grids, John Michell states in *View Over Atlantis,* "From what we have seen of the scientific methods practised by the adepts of the ancient world it is possible to draw two conclusions. First, they recognized the existence of some force or current, of whose potential we are ignorant, and discovered the form of natural science by which it could be manipulated. Secondly, they gained, apparently by means connected with their use of this current, certain direct insight into fundamental questions of philosophy, the nature of God and of the universe and the relationship between life and death."

Michell suggests that ancient civilizations were founded on the universal control of invisible force fields that encircle the globe, the fields of gravity and electromagnetic energy. He proposes that the efforts of scientists such as von Reichenbach and Wilhelm Reich "further confirms the possibility, indicated in vestigial folklore all over the world, that some form of natural energy was known in prehistoric times and that a method was discovered, involving a fusion of the terrestrial spirit with the solar spark by which this energy could be disposed to the benefit of the human race."

In *The Fairy Faith in Celtic Countries* W. Y. Evans-Wentz discusses the centers of terrestrial magnetic current:

". . . There seem to be certain favoured places on the earth where its magnetic and even more subtle forces are most powerful and most easily felt by persons susceptible to such things; and Carnoc appears to be one of the greatest of such places in Europe, and for this reason, as has been thought, was probably selected by its ancient priest-builders as the great centre for religious practices, for the celebration of pagan mysteries, for tribal assemblies, for astronomical observations, and very likely for establishing schools in which to educate neophytes for the priesthood. Tara with its tributary Boyne valley, is a similar place in Ireland."

John Michell points out that many great structures of the ancient world were constructed on the energy grids. "Yet the historical evidence suggests that these places were once considered merely of local importance and that all were subordinate to one great centre, the magical capital of the world," he states.

"If we accept the evidence for the former existence of a universal civilization, it must be assumed that the cataclysm that engulfed it, one of those recurring events by which the shape of continents is suddenly altered, disturbed the existing pattern of magnetic current and created a new terrestrial centre. With the former capital destroyed, perhaps submerged, the survivors of the disaster would first have located this place, and would there have erected a new powerful instrument as the first stage in re-establishing control over the earth's magnetic field. And here at the very centre of all the continents of the world we find the Great Pyramid."

The Great Pyramid is said to exist at the middle of the world because it is at the exact center of the earth's land mass. If lines are drawn through the north-south and east-west axis of the Great Pyramid, they equally divide the land mass of the world.

It may be that the ancient builders were aware of the energy currents and constructed the Great Pyramid at the center of the earth's land mass, as this was also the nucleus of the force fields. On the other hand, the Great Pyramid itself may have been the initiator or central generator of these invisible forces, and other pyramids, temples, and so on were located at strategic points to serve as relay stations. Either scheme provides some provocative possibilities. We have received a number of reports stating that the presence of a pyramid in a room changes the field.

"I expected to get results from experiments with pyramids and I have not been disappointed. However, I anticipated that any changes would occur inside the pyramid but did not expect the mere presence of the pyramid in a room to alter anything. But I swear the air is purer and more vibrant in that room. Our dog seeks out this room where he didn't before, and plants do better even though the amount of sunlight is no greater."

Information such as this seems to support the concept that the pyramid creates, enhances, or somehow captures unusual energy fields wherever it is located. If models of the Great Pyramid produce fields of some nature both within and beyond their perimeters, can we assume that the original does also? We have to remember, however, that research has demonstrated different results for experimental objects inside the pyramid and control objects outside the pyramid, and many of these objects were in close proximity to the pyramid. The forces outside may be there but of a more subtle quality, or perhaps different in unknown ways. While many tests have been run on the inside-versus-outside approach, little effort has been made to measure differences in phenomena with objects outside but next to pyramids and control objects, say, a block away.

Unusual phenomena have been reported atop the Great Pyramid, and likewise, experimenters with models have reported the presence of an energy field radiating from the apex. Clairvoyants claim they see a beam of light radiating upward to a distance equal to the height of the pyramid, and dowsers apparently pick up subtle increases of energy near the pyramid and amplified fields above the apex. Planes are instructed not to fly over the Gizeh pyramids as their instruments will go awry, and we have found that a compass held above the apex of a pyramid model will sometimes behave in an erratic fashion. That the compass will not always act in this manner might indicate a vacillation of force magnitude. The amount of energy inside the pyramid also changes from time to time such as may be found in the number of shaves from a razor blade, duration time for dehydration, plant movement, and so on. If it could be determined what variables are involved in this coming and going of energy, a big step would be taken toward defining the nature of the forces at play. Time of day, heat, humidity, light, season, weather, solar flare activity, and so forth may well be included as some of the variables influencing results, but these alone do not account for the differences.

Pyramids have been used to direct energy fields toward an object with some results. For example, a series of pyramids of equal size have been placed under beds to improve sleep and for therapeutic purposes. This use of pyramids is described in the chapters on "The Healing Phenomenon."

Energy generated inside a pyramid can be transferred outside by way of an agent which then acts much as the pyramid itself. Aluminum foil can be charged inside a pyramid and then be used as a wrapping for meat, vegetables, or other items. It seems to do as good a job of preserving food items as does the pyramid, although it loses its charge after a time. Metal plates have been used in a similar manner. We have found that water serves as one of the best storage systems for pyramid energy. Water seems to hold a charge for several days and can be used for drinking, bathing, watering plants, or whatever.

That a person could sit in a pyramid, soak up a charge and then share it with others, or scatter it about his environment like a good fairy depositing sunbeams didn't occur to us until we received the following note from Tom Garrett, Oklahoma City:

"I have come to believe that the energy generated in the pyramid can somehow attach itself to a person sitting in it and be transferred later to others. Example: One evening I had a terrible headache and headed for my pyramid. After a few minutes inside, my headache went away and I fell asleep for about thirty minutes. After waking I returned to the living room and reported my success to Mary, who at the time was suffering from cramps and a headache. I told her how I could still feel the area where the pain had been, but no pain was present. We discussed this for about five or ten minutes and I stood up to leave the room. It was at this point that Mary noticed that her cramps and headache had disappeared and she also reported being aware of the areas where the pain had been but was not anymore. During the period of time that we had been talking I had my arm around her shoulders and I believe that the physical contact might have been the deciding factor, if in fact there had been an energy transference."

The power of suggestion? This is possible, or the pain was psychosomatic in origin and was triggered to off position by means of the physical contact or through the discussion. It may simply have been a matter of the pain having run its course and the timing was coincidental. There are probably several explanations and we might have been tempted to select one of them had it not been that we started receiving shortly afterward similar reports from other people. Could it be that the energy generated by a natural healer such as Olga Worrall or Oskar Estebany is the same as that instilled in a person sitting inside a pyramid and when he leaves he can share this healing energy with others?

In Manly Palmer Hall's *The Secret Teachings of All Ages* we find the following statement in regard to the initiations within the Great Pyramid: "With the giving of the Name, the new initiate became himself a pyramid, within the chambers of whose soul numberless other human beings might also receive spiritual enlightenment."

Our imagination takes hold at this point. If, we wonder, it is possible to inoculate an individual with the positive qualities of pyramid energy—tranquillity, health, peacefulness—and he is able to share these desirable properties with others, what changes could be brought about in the home, neighborhood, community, nation, world if we could get enough people to start the yeasting process? Is it possible that the pyramid was designed with this mission in mind?

That special places exist is nowhere more visible than within pyramid space itself.

"I have built an eight-foot-tall pyramid in my back yard where I have been conducting experiments with plants. One day I had to make a quick trip to town and left the door of the pyramid open. When I returned, my big Labrador was lying inside. There was nothing inside to attract him. It was a hot day but rather than lie in the cool of the shade he chose the pyramid in which the sun

Early stage in construction of 16-foot pyramid. One side of pyramid was aligned North-South by means of a compass and correction made for declination.

South side of outdoor pryamid.

was heating through. Several times I have caught him pawing at the door in an effort to open it."

Soon after we completed our eleven-foot pyramid our two German shepherds laid claim to it. They sniffed all around inside and finally settled on the northeast corner. They have abandoned their long-established nests in a comfortable shed in favor of the pyramid, and they always go to the northeast corner. We didn't consider this as being particularly unusual until we started hearing from others.

"Both my cat and my dog show an extreme interest in being near my pyramid. After I had constructed the pyramid, my cat would go to the garage door and howl to be let in. This is very unusual for until the pyramid was there the cat would only make gestures of wanting outside (never to go to the garage). I do not allow my dog inside the pyramid due to experiments within, but she shows a desire to lie near it. She always lies at the northeast corner —never anywhere else."

We have now heard similar stories from a number of people. One friend who had this experience tried to confuse his dog. The dog had discovered the northeast corner but the friend, knowing that once a dog has picked his spot and left his odor there, will normally always return to it, rotated the pyramid so that the northeast corner became the southwest corner. He watched as his dog entered, sniffed around the pyramid, picked up his own odor in the southwest corner, hesitated a moment, and then went to the northeast corner and lay down.

An animal's sensitivity to special places is noted by Lyall Watson in *Super Nature:*

"The choice of a resting place naturally has to be made very carefully with regard to warmth and shelter and safety from predators, but often an animal will choose a place that seems to be far less appealing on these grounds than another only a short distance away. Domestic dogs and cats show the same behavior, and their owners know full well that it is no good making this decision on the pet's behalf—they have to wait until the animal chooses its own place and then put the sleeping basket there. There are some places on which an animal will not lie on any account."

An animal apparently knows that where there are special places there are also places—as Carlos Castaneda learned—that are foreboding and must be avoided. Not too surprising, then, that pyramids would also have high and low fields.

"I have found evidence to the effect that the interior southwest corner of a pyramid model may be far from beneficial," Tom Garrett noted in the log he turned over to us. "Example: During one of my experiments I had cut an apple in two and placed one half inside the pyramid and one half outside. After only a few hours the outside apple had turned dark brown color where the inside apple (at the King's Chamber level) had remained white and moist. After two days the inside apple showed only slight darkening while the one outside was very dark and shriveled. I wanted to take a nap in the pyramid and moved the apple from the King's Chamber level to get it out of my way. I placed it in the southwest corner to make room for myself. After a period of forty-five minutes I was rested and ready to return to the house. When I moved the apple back to the King's Chamber level, I was stunned at its appearance. It had turned very brown, almost to the extent of the control apple outside. In less than two hours a mold had appeared on the inside apple and at this point I removed it from the pyramid. The control apple did not develop a mold for another two days."

It is interesting to note in the January-February 1975 issue of *The Pyramid Guide* Bill Cox relates that when Bill Kerrell ran tests of different locations inside a pyramid with a magnetic field analyzer that the "lowest indication appeared at (b) SW corner."

Continuing his findings regarding the southwest corner, Garrett stated, "Several weeks later, I was in the pyramid with a friend and somehow I had positioned myself so that my head was in the southwest corner. After a few minutes I noticed a pressure on my head that culminated in a slight headache. I repositioned myself more towards the center and the pressure ceased. I have tricked others into this area and they reported a slight pressure and repositioned themselves. I would do this by getting in the pyramid first and only leaving them room in the southwest area."

On one occasion during August 1975 Garrett watched as droplets of water formed on the southwest corner of the outside of the pyramid. The building, including the roof, was completely dry at the time, nor had there been any rain earlier. The droplets have not appeared since that time, he said.

We conducted an experiment with sixteen persons. One at a time they were taken inside an outdoor pyramid. The door was shut and they were turned about in order to disorient them. They were then told to face in the direction that seemed "ideal" to them. Fourteen of the sixteen faced east. This, incidentally, was the direction in which the initiates of the Mystery Schools were placed when going through out-of-the-body experiences. A friend who is considered an authority on the Plains Indians told us that the tepees were always faced to the east.

"I asked him if each of the two spots had a special name. He said that the good one was called the sitio and the bad one the enemy; he said these two places were the key to a man's well-being, especially for a man who was pursuing knowledge . . ."—from *The Teachings of Don Juan.*

13

The Dweller Within

The shape of the future . . . this is the way we speculated several years ago when we started researching pyramids. In every direction that we turned in our experiments new and exciting discoveries unfolded before us. "The Great Pyramid may have been one of the Seven Wonders of the Ancient World," we found ourselves saying, "but its progeny will become one of the wonders of the modern one."

We told friends and acquaintances—occasionally an audience—that by 1980 we would start seeing homes constructed in the traditional pyramid shape, aligned on the north-south axis and fully ready for people to live happily ever after. We proved to be underachievers as prophets, for that world of tomorrow is with us today. Already pyramid homes are being constructed; a large pyramid church is serving an overflow crowd of attendants; a large pyramid office building is being planned in Washington, D.C., and smaller offices already exist; pyramid recreational shelters are in operation; backyard experimental models are growing larger and larger, some serving dual roles as storage sheds; and pyramid doghouses and greenhouses are no longer news.

Should we risk prophesying again we might venture that the trend to pyramid-shaped buildings is not a fad, that we are witnessing only the initial gestures of a movement that will continue to grow. People who spend $60,00 for a home or many times that for an office building are not interested in fads; they make their plans with some solid reasoning behind them.

Some of these reasons are obvious. For one thing, they are finally listening, at least indirectly, to Buckminster Fuller, inventor of the geodesic dome among other things, who stated many years ago that we shouldn't live or work in cubes. He said that right-angled walls and ceilings inhibited the easy flow of energy fields and that we were being bombarded by distorted forces. This principle would seem to have been demonstrated by the construction of a hospital in Saskatchewan, Canada, with trapezoidal rooms and irregular corridors that reportedly has better patient-recovery statistics than neighboring institutions.

Karl Drbal, the Czechoslovakian radio engineer credited with discovering that pyramid models sharpen razor blades, told Sheila Ostrander and Lynn Schroeder, authors of *Psychic Discoveries Behind the Iron Curtain,* that the forms in which we spend much of our lives influence our health and that the sphere and pyramid have beneficial effects. Drbal's conclusions were based on many years of researching the influence of shapes and forms on a variety of objects. Our research with plants and small animals tends to confirm this position. Plants placed in pyramids thrive and grow more rapidly than those outside, and definitely more so than those placed inside cubes. When our gerbil was housed inside a pyramid, she appeared contented, ate, looked and kept her nest organized and neat. When her cage was placed inside a cube of the same material and volume as the pyramid, she appeared nervous, picked at her food, and scattered her nest about the cage. She was inside the same cage in both instances.

Occasionally people point out that most pyramid models are housed within cube-shaped rooms and doesn't this affect the field within the pyramid? It's a good question and one that has not been adequately examined at this writing. However, we have conducted a number of tests with water, milk, food, subjective states, and so on in order to draw comparisons between outside pyramids and those placed in rectangular or cube-shaped rooms. We have not been able to find any noticeable differences. We found the results curious . . . we had expected to discover measurable differences. We did find, however, that pyramids placed in a room with a large amount of circuitry or metal sheeting did not perform as satisfactorily as those in rooms where these conditions did not exist. People sometimes report no noticeable results from their pyramids. Upon checking, we have learned their experiments have been conducted in rooms loaded with circuitry and metal. This is one of the problems faced by most laboratories.

This may be one of the reasons, incidentally, that psychic sensitives sometimes have problems performing under laboratory conditions: their frequencies may be in conflict or overwhelmed by the electric and electromagnetic fields present in the room. Some individuals with paranormal powers refuse to demonstrate their skills in laboratory settings for this reason. As our cells, tissues, organs, bodies radiate energy and are in turn influenced by the frequencies and force fields around us, it makes us wonder to what extent we are being manipulated by the electrical circuitry, radio and television waves, steel, iron, and so forth that constantly surround and bombard us. Maybe the reason that we like to get out in the open and claim that we feel better when we do is not just a matter of exercise but is also partly to free ourselves from congested frequencies.

When pyramids have failed to work, we have suggested

that they be moved to another room or building and this usually takes care of the problem.

When electrical circuitry, the presence of metal, and so on are not issues, we have noticed little difference in the results of inside and outside pyramids. Inasmuch as all rooms have some electrical circuitry and metal, it would seem that at certain levels the pyramid is not affected; above this level it is. This apparently being the case, it would follow that this difference would not occur sharply but would happen according to degrees. The conclusion that one is forced to reach, therefore, is that inside pyramids are to some extent affected by their immediate environment. It may be that alterations occur as a result of a combination of influencing factors. For example, the mere presence of electrical lines might have little effect; it might be the voltage, amperage, type of wire insulation, number of outlets, types of instruments or appliances being operated in the vicinity, pattern of the wiring around the room, and so forth. More research is required in order to learn what the influencing factors are.

In many ways, pyramids give indications of being complete within themselves—that is, they seem to create their own environment. While their effectiveness can be inhibited by an overload of electric or electromagnetic forces, on the other hand we have not been very successful in amplifying results. We have tried using pyramids within pyramids, pyramids within spheres and cones, and vice versa, but have found little difference in the results. Evidently the pyramid has a certain optimal level at which it captures, enhances, or generates energy and it cannot be substantially increased beyond that amount.

Several experimenters have endeavored to increase the energy field within pyramids by lining them with copper sheets or using capstones of various materials. When differences have been noticed, they are usually attributed to the subjective reactions of persons sitting, sleeping, or meditating inside of pyramids. The differences may be real enough but, of course, it is difficult to measure subjective states. Monitoring of physiological conditions, pulse, galvanistic skin response, heart rate, brainwaves, and so forth reveals little if any measurable difference between, say, a pyramid composed entirely of wood and one that has a copper-lined capstone. Comparisons of psycho-physiological states produced inside as against those produced outside are discussed in the chapter on "Experiments."

But there is another reason for constructing buildings in the pyramid shape. It is an exceptionally strong structural form. On every hand, from meteorologists, climatologists, astronomers, and prophets, we are hearing that our weather is changing, that it is likely to become more violent and erratic during the next few years—hurricanes, tornadoes, droughts followed by flooding, and so on. Recent articles in several national magazines quote eminent scientists as saying the weather is no longer predictable. Some ecologists are saying that our abuse of natural resources, pollution, the bombarding of space with noise, and a variety of radio waves have destroyed natural balances, the consequence being that nature is upset, therefore unpredictable. True or not, these warnings have prompted some people to explore various types of construction that can withstand harsh weather conditions. The pyramid would seem to meet this test. It has no horizontal surfaces to expose to wind, rain, hail, or snow.

Although buildings constructed in the pyramid shape are impervious to most weather conditions, this would not appear to be one of the reasons for the construction of the original pyramids. However, investigations of the Great Pyramid revealed that it has more than likely survived a number of hefty earthquakes. In relatively modern history this includes the earthquake of the late thirteenth century that destroyed Cairo. It was following this earthquake that the polished veneer was stripped from the Great Pyramid and used to construct new buildings, including the mosque of Sultan Hasan in 1356. Evidently the architects of the Great Pyramid provided for such natural catastrophes in the design, as Peter Tompkins states in *Secrets of the Great Pyramid:*

"Davidson [David Davidson, an English structural engineer] says the five construction chambers were especially designed to take a considerable impact. Instead of resting the uppermost beams on a hard granite wall, the builders rested them on limestone, which could more easily crush and flow in case of subsidence, taking the strain off the lower rows of rafters and keeping the walls of the King's Chamber intact. Davidson says that a more rigid design, uniform from the lowest to the highest chamber, would have been disastrous.

"To permit this buffer effect being fully developed, rafters of the chambers were not tied into the east and west walls. Instead two immense limestone walls, wholly outside of, and independent of all the granite floors and supporting blocks, were built on the east and west sides. As Petrie [William Flinders Petrie, nineteenth century English mathematician and surveyor] put it: 'Between these great walls all the chambers stand, unbonded and capable of yielding freely to settlement.' "

This construction applies, of course, only to the Great Pyramid, and, in this case we are considering a structure built wholly of stone. That the pyramid shape itself contributes to resistance of damage from earthquakes, nuclear explosions, and so on does not necessarily follow.

As mentioned elsewhere in this book and in *The Secret Power of Pyramids,* pyramid research has not reached a sufficient plateau of sophistication to determine differences in materials used in the construction of pyramid models. So, at this point, we continue to say that one can use almost anything in the way of material with the exception of metal. However, we have been told that the builders of the Great Pyramid were careful in their selection of the stone, some of it being transported six hundred miles. The question raised is whether the stone was selected because of its size, strength, and so on or were there other criteria? One also wonders if the builders would have used other materials if they had been available, or was the stone the perfect material?

It is known that granite such as that used in the King's Chamber does produce a piezoelectric effect when placed under pressure. Did the builders use the granite slabs to produce an electrical charge or was their selection based only on appearance and strength? Any number of books have been written about the unusual properties of stone. The following words from *The Etheric Double* by A. E. Powell refer primarily to precious stones but it makes one wonder if other stones do not have some unique properties:

"Precious stones, being the highest development of the mineral kingdom, have very great power of receiving and retaining impressions . . . On the other hand, gems may be a powerful reservoir of good and desirable influence. Thus, for example, the Gnostic gems employed in Initiation ceremonies two thousand years ago retain even to this day powerful magnetic influence. Some Egyptian scarabaei are still effective, though much older even than the Gnostic gems."

New York psychiatrist Dr. John Pierrakos has done extensive research on the energy pulsations of man, animals, plants, and minerals. In the monograph "The Energy Field in Man and Nature," he described the vibrations of various crystals. He also discusses the pulsation of trees and points out that evergreens have a vibration similar to that of the human body. Further research, then, may reveal that indeed it does make a difference what kind of materials, or even the species of wood, for example, are used in pyramid construction.

Although a great deal remains to be learned about building materials, the shape of the pyramid and its alignment have been standardized. Pyramid models must follow the shape and the north-south alignment of the Great Pyramid in order to be effective. To the extent that these properties are distorted, so accordingly are the results. Why the shape is sacred is not entirely known. The shape lends itself to a great deal of symbolical meaning, as do the internal and external measurements, which provide considerable mathematical information. For example, if you take the height of the pyramid as the radius of a circle, the circumference of this circle is equal to the circumference of the square base of the pyramid. Any other pyramid shape would not produce this formula. For those interested in the fascinating study of the mathematics of the Great Pyramid, two excellent sources are *Secrets of the Great Pyramid* by Peter Tompkins and *The View Over Atlantis* by John Michell.

We might remind ourselves that the sides of the Great Pyramid are not equilateral triangles although they come close to being. If the sides were equilateral triangles, then the energy fields would likely be reflected in a more limited and definitive pattern, whereas being slightly changed from having the sides the same length as the base the energy flow would move along a constantly altered pathway.

It should also be remembered that the sides of the Great Pyramid are slightly indented. As this indentation amounts to slightly more than thirty inches, it is not noticeable unless special lines of sight are taken. Petrie was the first to call this fact to attention and it was later to be confirmed in an aerial photograph taken by Brigadier P. R. C. Groves, the British prophet of air power. It can be assumed that this distortion also alters the reflection of energy fields, wavelengths, and so on, but we have no way of knowing whether this was a purpose of the builders. We indented the side slightly in our outdoor twelve-foot pyramid but at this writing we do not know what effect if any it will have on our experimental results. Whatever the purpose of the original builders of the Great Pyramid, their design certainly appears to be the correct one for producing pyramid energy fields.

While many shapes remain to be explored and the work in this particular field actually has only begun, anyone building a large and expensive structure might be ill-advised to alter the design unless he does so for the sake of research. Such alterations would include placing a structure beneath the pyramid shape, attaching rooms to the outside, dormer-type windows or entrances extending from the outside, protruding bay windows, and so forth. Such changes constitute a different shape and may distort the original field. The distortion might be very slight, of course, and perhaps even beneficial, but these issues should be kept in mind when planning construction.

In the chapter "A Special Place" we discussed the existence of certain places that apparently have enriched or unique energy fields. Investigations from time to time point to the special fields generated by churches, temples, shrines, and so on.

"Great shrines are usually erected on the spot where holy men lived, where some great event, such as an Initiation, took place, or where there is a relic of a great person. In any of these cases a powerful magnetic centre of influence has been created which will persist for thousands of years," Powell states in his book mentioned earlier.

And Michell states in *View Over Atlantis,* "The practice of locating sacred centres in accordance with the flow of terrestrial magnetic current was not confined to prehistoric times, for it appears that every Christian church was similarly sited. The orientation of a church, even its dimensions and architectural plan, was determined by the lines of current, of which the strongest spring is frequently located directly beneath its tower. At this spot the celestial influences, attracted by the spire, combine with the terrestrial force to produce the fusion."

In view of these findings it is interesting to note that pyramids apparently leave behind them a certain charge or unique energy field. Dowsers claim they can pick up the spot where a pyramid has sat for any length of time. Birds have been noticed to gather on spots where outside pyramids once were located, and we have observed our

The pyramid-shaped Unity Church of Christianity. The pyramid helps meditation.

dogs coming back time and again, days apart, to sniff at such locations.

"For about three months I had a wooden pyramid sitting several hundred feet away from our house," a San Francisco correspondent wrote. "I used it for experiments but tore it down when I decided to build a larger one nearer to the house. One day I noticed that my spaniel was lying on this particular spot. I didn't think too much about it until he kept going back there. He kept this up until my other pyramid was completed and then he started lying beside it."

The investigation of unusual energy fields by shapes and forms has led Benson Herbert, director of Paraphysical Laboratories in England, to speculate about the relation of architecture to poltergeists. Sheila Ostrander and Lynn Schroeder quote Herbert as considering "the possibility of designing a poltergeist house, of such a shape as to encourage paranormal incidents, a kind of scientific 'House that Jack Built,' incorporating architectural features that I have seen in certain 'haunted' Scottish castles; I visualize these shapes as hypergeometrical sections."

But the haunting for most people who have experienced pyramid space has been limited to feelings of peace, vitality, seclusion, rest, healing, and spiritual awakening. These were the qualities sought by the congregation of Unity Church of Christianity in Houston, Texas.

The new church building, which opened its doors in August 1973, was the vision of its minister, the Reverend John Rankin. The October 1975 issue of *Houston, Home and Garden* stated, "The congregation had grown so fast that a new building was needed. Plans floundered until Rankin's powerful vision of a golden pyramid came to him. 'Ministering at the central altar,' he recalls in a recent book, 'was a high priest serving healing and communion.' Rankin says he felt impelled to share this experience with the building committee despite a lifelong skepticism of anything visionary. Today, Rankin's

Artist's drawing of pyramid home.

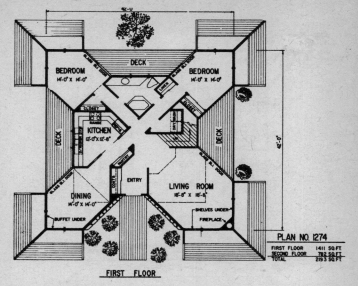

FIRST FLOOR

PLAN NO. 1274

FIRST FLOOR	1411 SQ.FT.
SECOND FLOOR	782 SQ.FT.
TOTAL	2193 SQ.FT.

First floor of pyramid model home.

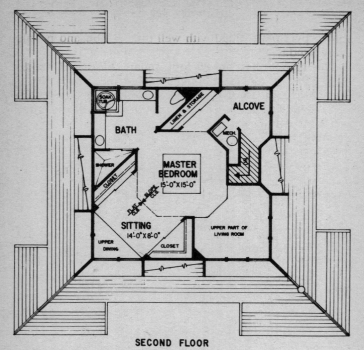

SECOND FLOOR

Second floor of pyramid model home.

golden pyramid is filled with well over a thousand people every Sunday . . ."

The church has an 89-foot square base and stands over 63 feet tall. A staff member of the Burde Baker Planetarium in Houston helped align the structure on the north-south axis. Rankin told us that the new church building doubled the seating capacity of the previous building but that attendance had increased so rapidly that they are not able to seat the crowds even with extra folding chairs in the aisles. He has received inquiries from other ministers of many different denominations from most of the states and several foreign countries.

To our knowledge, the largest pyramid house will be constructed near Oklahoma City, Oklahoma. We received a telephone call one day from a young couple who said they were planning to build a true pyramid home and they wanted to visit with us. We spent a fascinating evening with Mr. and Mrs. Smith discussing pyramid phenomena and their exciting plans to build their home on thirty wooded acres and beside their privately owned lake. At this writing, the house is under construction and will have a 60-foot base. It will tower nearly 40 feet and will be topped with a glass capstone.

They invited us to contact the firm that provided the plans for the house. Several telephone conversations and correspondence followed with Heritage Homes Plan Service, Inc., of Atlanta, Georgia, and we learned that the company has sold 102 plan sets to persons in a number of states, Canada, and Ireland.

The exterior is finished in lapped siding, but it can be finished with shingles, fiberglass or other low-maintenance material. Stone veneer is used around the front door.

Each corner of the first floor of the pyramid contains one room. A deck is placed between each of the corner rooms, which have five walls. Two are bedrooms, one is a living room, and the fourth is a dining area. The entry hall, pantry, kitchen, utility area, stairs, and a full bath are in the central portion of the main floor. The living room is two stories high with a fireplace in one corner. All the major rooms on the first floor open to covered decks.

The entire second floor is a master-bedroom suite. The bedroom itself is in the center of the pyramid. A bath with both shower and Oriental soak-tub takes up one pyramid corner.

With the kind of evidence gleaned from the various experiments, what kind of results can we expect from sustained exposure to pyramid space? It is exciting to speculate on this when we pause to reflect that not only will the pyramid householder be subjected to pyramid energy many hours each day and night but also will his food, clothes, and all of his personal items.

We really don't know what the result will be. The pyramid dwellers have cast themselves in courageous roles. They are the pioneers and from them we will learn more than we ever could otherwise. Will their physical, mental, and spiritual growth be so in evidence and so attractive to the rest of us that pyramids will revolutionize the building trade? Or will their homes someday be abandoned, standing empty and haunted, collecting superstition and myths with the passing years? Will the children of today's pyramid dwellers be seen by future historians as the genesis of a superior race of man, or will they be tomorrow's misfits? Will pyramid dwellers respond to their fellow men with new-found love, maturity, charity, or will they find the environment beyond their prism paradise faded in comparison and become recluses shut off from a world they would rather not face? Such thoughts are exciting; they are also frightening.

How should these houses be designed? What rooms, what activities, should be planned for particular locations of the structure? All activities can't take place in the middle of the pyramid, the King's Chamber, or near the apex. What about our experiments with plants, with food items . . . do these tell us anything? Should we pay attention to the energy-level readings of dowsers? What about the less desirable effects produced by the southwest corner? the northeast corner where animals prefer to lie?

The evidence to date would indicate that the pyramid works for man's benefit. It is interesting to note that persons with claustrophobia have remarked that they never feel this way inside a pyramid regardless of how snugly fitting it may be.

But many of our questions must await answers that only continuous exposure to the powers of the pyramid can supply. Through what doors will they pass to bring us the answers?

14

Experiments: The Lab Confirms

The laboratory reports rested on the desk in front of us. Seven long days we had waited for these reports and the moment of truth was at hand. It really wasn't that, we told ourselves . . . if the results were positive, we would have to explain that not a great deal of significance can be placed on one series of tests with only four subjects; if negative, it would be necessary for us to argue that there were many variables to be considered, things would have to be checked out, more tests run.

"We really can't imply too much one way or the other," we said to each other. And the echo was always, "That's true, but . . ." Yet it was with the "but" that we got hung up emotionally and we couldn't shake the feeling that these tests were important to us. Say what we would to others, we could not deny that we were looking for some kind of confirmation. This was countdown, and all of the hundreds of tests that might follow, all of the statistical gleanings that would have to be done before others could say that the tests were significant were shadows lingering in the wings. Our minds said the reports would show at best "directions for research," but our hearts knew the answer would or would not be there.

Perhaps we needed that gesture of confirmation much as the religious devotee comes upon those moments of questioning when he asks for a sign. How long we had worked with pyramids, time and again getting results of some sort and not always expected, so that we had come to develop a faith in the pyramid's strange powers. But always the Doubting Thomas within us queried how an ordinary box, whatever its shape, could uniquely affect its contents.

So our sign on this occasion was to be the pyramid's ability to alter certain physiological states of the human body. The tests were to consist of before-and-after pyramid exposure measurements of skin temperature, Kirlian photos of fingerpads, and a series of blood tests, including trace minerals. The tests were to be conducted by a highly respected medical doctor and researcher and the samples were to be submitted to a well-equipped laboratory.

Our expectations and anxieties undoubtedly mounted because of the lapse of time that occurred from the day we made arrangements for the tests to the day they were carried out. So we worried the results into greater proportions than they undoubtedly deserved, but it does little good to argue with oneself in such situations. It was hold-the-breath time for us.

Many experiments had led up to this point. We had experienced and had so many people report of changes in mental and physical states as a result of pyramid exposure. Many common denominators had emerged in the process of people reporting of their experiments with healing. These were occasionally supported by physicians and hospital reports. The presence of unusual energy fields had been monitored in solids, liquids, plants, insects, animals, as well as humans, by a variety of techniques. We had explored energy fields as understood in Western physics, as conceptualized by Eastern references to prana and unified field theories, and the investigation of psi phenomena. We were familiar with magic-wand reports, the use of dowsing devises to measure energy levels inside pyramids. We had decided that dowsing techniques, while interesting and undoubtedly useful, were primarily of a subjective nature inasmuch as the operator was part of the circuit. The results rested too much on the abilities of the experimenter rather than on effects produced by the pyramids.

These things were behind us when we decided to run the series of physiological tests that could be examined in the laboratory.

Previous to this, I (Schul) had spent more than three years in the study of nutritional therapy, bioelectrical medicine, the use of Kirlian photography as a diagnostic tool, and so on. These investigations allowed me to make the acquaintance of Dr. Hugh Riordan, a Wichita, Kansas, psychiatrist. He offered to run the physiological tests and we readily accepted.

Early on the morning of December 14, 1975, Dr. Riordan, Brenda Scott, and Lowanda Cady, Dr. Riordan's assistants who are familiar with research procedures, and myself drove to Ed Pettit's home, where he had recently constructed a wooden sixteen-foot-base pyramid in his backyard. As it was the largest one that we had constructed, we decided to use it for the experiments. In tow were the necessary instruments for taking blood samples, including a centrifuge, a portable Kirlian camera using Polaroid film, and a skin-temperature machine.

It was a mild sunny day and we decided to do the before-pyramid tests on the lawn near the pyramid. We decided to use four subjects, Cady, Scott, and the two of us. Kirlian photos were taken of the fingertips of the dominant hand of each subject; skin-temperature levels were recorded; and the blood samples drawn. Each of us then spent fifteen minutes alone in the pyramid, and then, while still inside the pyramid, the same tests were again taken.

Two of the measurements, of course, were immediately available—the skin-temperature readings and the Kirlian photos. The skin-temperature differences were as follows:

	Before	*After*
Cady	88.3°	90.3°
Scott	77.8°	79.1°
Pettit	89.0°	76.4°
Schul	88.4°	76.8°

Cady's skin temperature increased 2.0 degrees; Scott's increased 1.3 degrees; Pettit's decreased 12.6 degrees; and Schul's decreased 11.6 degrees. We are not sure why the skin temperature of the two females increased slightly whereas the skin temperature of the males showed a sharp decrease. The two females had not been exposed to pyramid space prior to the experiment, whereas the males had. More than likely, however, the differences can be attributed to the sudden change in the temperature of the air. The "before" temperature of all four subjects were taken when the air was warm, but after the inside-pyramid readings were taken of the two females, the wind made a rapid switch from the south to the north and the temperature took an eleven-degree dive within ten minutes. As this was approximately the same difference as the skin-temperature drop in the two males, whose inside readings were taken after the temperature change, this would be the logical reason. It was unfortunate that the change in the weather occurred during this time. Because of this it would be difficult to draw any conclusions from the Pettit and Schul readings. However, both Cady and Scott produced a higher skin temperature inside the pyramid, indicating more relaxed states.

The Kirlian photos revealed some interesting differences and we were not disappointed in the results. Photos, of course, explain themselves much better than verbal de-

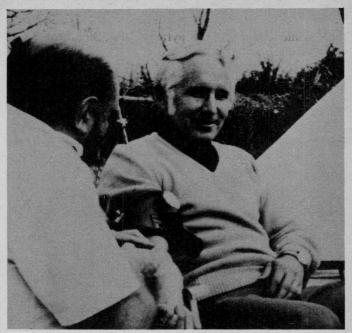

Dr. Riordan drawing blood sample from Bill Schul outside pyramid.

scriptions. Pictures taken after fifteen minutes in the pyramid were brighter, the edges of the corona were less frayed, the dendrites were sharper, and the pattern was unbroken.

The brighter auras would seem to indicate a greater amount of energy and balance. A comparison between the before-and-after photos was similar to those drawn between the aura of a person suffering from some illness or fatigue and the aura following successful treatment. High-frequency pictures of fingertips taken prior to and following auricular therapy reveal the presence of greater energy radiation and a balance of pattern after the administration of treatment. Pictures similar to these are produced before and after pyramid exposure.

Judging from Kirlian photos of the fingertips of persons suffering from pathological conditions, emotional or mental stress, or fatigue, as compared to fingertips of healthy, undisturbed individuals, the less frayed edges and sharper dendrites would seem to indicate healthier, less tense, and more balanced states. These comparisons would also seem to apply to before-and-after pyramid exposure states.

The French physician P. Nogier has administered magnetic stimulation to acupuncture points in the ear and produced some fascinating before-and-after pictures. These reveal a much higher light radiation following the treatment. It is interesting to note the similarities between this set of photos and those produced via the pyramid. One wonders, then, if the nature of the stimulation is similar. If so, this would indicate that a portion of the force field produced inside the pyramid is of an increased magnetic field.

In the monograph "Bioelectronics" Nobel Prize winner Albert Szent-Gyorgy suggests a different approach to the examination of matter than by means of the particle. He states that the study of energy would be more fruitful and offers the hypothesis that the flow of electrons from molecule to molecule may be responsible for maintaining

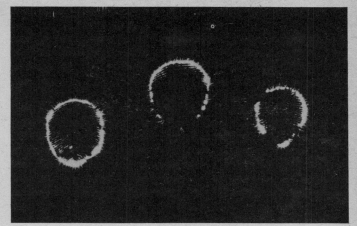

Fingerprints of subject holding plates before plates were charged in a pyramid.

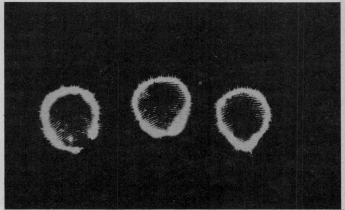

Fingerprints of subject holding plates after plates were charged in a pyramid.

the patterns of matter that we call tissue, muscles, organs, and bodies.

Additional light is thrown on this subject by Dr. E. H. Frei, director of the Department of Electronics at the Weizmann Institute. He explains that studies have shown that magnetic fields do affect cells, tissues, and so on. "No rigorous theories exist to explain these magnetic effects although rough analyses show that they would be very small in fields up to several thousand gauss. However, one can assume that in biological systems even very small effects could accumulate and cause significant changes," he states in an article, "Medical Applications of Magnetism," published in the October 1972 issue of *Bulletin of the Atomic Scientists.*

Dr. Frei discusses work with muscle stimulation, explaining that "results show that practically all muscles will contract as the magnetic field on them is altered . . . an electric field produced by a changing magnetic field can send a current through a cell and in this way stimulate all kinds of muscles." Dr. Frei suggests that this approach might be used in the stimulation of the cortex. "There is hope that by employing properly designed time-varying magnetic fields one could stimulate phenomena in the brain which otherwise can only be produced by inserting electrodes below the skull."

In 1938 G. C. Kimball reported differences in growth rates of yeast cultures exposed to magnetic fields. And in 1946 J. Magrou and P. Manigault produced abnormal growth rate in plants with magnetic fields. Of the latter research, Dr. Frei stated in the above mentioned article, ". . . The data given on the pole face geometry indicates high gradient values. Comparison with control plants is quite remarkable . . ." These phenomena are also produced inside pyramids.

It was with the blood tests, however, that we obtained the most startling results. The differences are difficult to believe—that we could run blood tests outside the pyramid and a few minutes later take the same tests and obtain readings with considerable variation is an amazing experience. At this time we cannot provide a great deal in the way of interpretation. To attempt to do so might be misleading, for the series of tests need to be taken many times with a large number of subjects. Actually, the tests speak for themselves anyway. We might add that exposure to the pyramid tends to bring the readings to within the normal range or, when already within the normal range, more toward the center of this range. It would seem that the pyramid works to bring the processes of the body into balance. In some instances, however, it does not and it would be difficult to say without additional research whether this is due to individual differences in biochemistry—of which the range is wide, according to Dr. Roger Williams, biochemist at the University of Texas at Austin—or whether these readings are temporary stages in adjustment of the body, and so on. Clearly, the differences are there and warrant further investigation. Within the concepts of the holistic approach to man, any interpretation of what is happening to the blood as a result of pyramid exposure should not be attempted within only a mechanical-chemical framework. All functions of the body—physical, chemical, electrical, emotional, mental, and spiritual—should not be considered separately but as components of an integrated dynamic system. Whereas we may say today that such-and-such is the normal range for a certain reading, perhaps tomorrow we will qualify this by adding "under certain conditions."

After examining many reports regarding medical application of the effects of magnetic fields, Dr. Frei stated, ". . . One is struck by the diverse and what sometimes seem to be incredible findings, such as one which reports on wound healings by magnets. On the other hand, other research appears to be more fully documented. One paper reports that the growth of certain tumors is delayed or inhibited, while another work describes how agglutination times of erythrocytes as well as blood coagulation times may be affected to some extent by magnetic fields."

Following are the before-and-after blood-test results:

LOWANDA CADY

	Normal Range	Before	After
White blood count	5–10,000 cu. mm	9,600	8,300
Red blood count	4–6,000,000 cu. mm	4,530,000	4,240,000
Hemoglobin	12–17 gm/dl	14.3	13.4
Hematocrit	37–52%	43	40
Differential			
Segmented	50–70%	42	33
Bands	0–5%	1	..
Lymphocytes	20–40%	51	64
Monocytes	1–6%	6	3
Eosinophils	1–5%	..	..
Blood Serum			
Copper	1.00 parts per million	1.24	1.08
Zinc	1.00 parts per million	1.00	1.00
Iron	1.20 parts per million	1.20	1.08
Glucose	65–110	91	125

BRENDA SCOTT

	Normal Range	Before	After
White blood count	5–10,000 cu. mm	6,500	4,000
Red blood count	4–6,000,000 cu. mm	3,920,000	3,960,000
Hemoglobin	12–17 gm/dl	11.4	11.6
Hematocrit	37–52%	35	35
Differential			
Segmented	50–70%	52	42
Bands	0–5%	1	..
Lymphocytes	20–40%	41	48
Monocytes	1–6%	3	8
Eosinophils	1–5%	3	2
Blood Serum			
Copper	1.00 parts per million	2.84	2.86
Zinc	1.00 parts per million	0.80	1.12
Iron	1.20 parts per million	0.56	0.66
Glucose	65–110	76	77

ED PETTIT

	Normal Range	Before	After
White blood count	5–10,000 cu. mm	5,900	6,300
Red blood count	4–6,000,000 cu. mm	4,640,000	4,460,000
Hemoglobin	12–17 gm/dl	14.8	14.2
Hematocrit	37–52%	44	42
Differential			
Segmented	50–70%	47	55
Bands	0–5%	..	..
Lymphocytes	20–40%	43	42
Monocytes	1–6%	9	1
Eosinophils	1–5%	1	2
Blood Serum			
Copper	1.10 parts per million	1.53	1.32
Zinc	1.00 parts per million	0.97	1.04
Iron	1.20 parts per million	0.70	0.58
Glucose	65–110	96	88

BILL SCHUL

	Normal Range	Before	After
White blood count	5–10,000 cu. mm	9,300	9,400
Red blood count	4–6,000,000 cu. mm	4,890,000	4,990,000
Hemoglobin	12–17 gm/dl	14.5	15.0
Hematocrit	37–52%	44	45
Differential			
Segmented	50–70%	49	63
Bands	0–5%	..	..
Lymphocytes	20–40%	42	30
Monocytes	1–6%	4	4
Eosinophils	1–5%	5	3
Blood Serum			
Copper	1.10 parts per million	1.14	1.18
Zinc	1.00 parts per million	1.00	1.34
Iron	1.20 parts per million	0.46	0.98
Glucose	65–110	79	84

Making Kirlian photos of subject's fingers inside
16-foot pyramid.

Immediately after the tests were completed, Lowanda Cady found a corner in which to be alone and she wrote down her experiences while inside the pyramid—her first. It is an interesting account and reflects the subjective state an individual can experience while inside a pyramid. She was kind enough to allow us to include it in this chapter:

"A lamp had been placed inside the pyramid and I found the light to be totally intrusive. I turned my chair so that the light was behind me and I was facing north. The light seemed not to come from behind me but to be an encompassing distraction. I got up and turned off the light, felt my way back to the chair and was immediately aware of sound. The insulation of the pyramid, responding to the thirty-knot wind outside, cracked and snapped. It sounded like sand hitting the floor all around me. I was afraid. I rebelled against the fear—isolating its probable source. Too many Egyptian-mummy spook shows made me feel I had to guard against being transported through time to some ancient past. Quickly, the fear was gone. Never did any feeling of disquiet return. Though I was not able to relegate the sound to the exterior, it remained a sound that was close by me.

"My eyes were closed, and I usually can visualize easily just by closing my eyes. But mostly imagery eluded me. Briefly, swirling sand dunes would flash into my closed vision. The majority of the time I was aware of looking through miles and miles of darkness. I thought I could, if I elected to do so, see an image at the end of the darkness—when I would agree to allow the image to come through, bright flashes of light seemed to flare at the outside edge of my vision. Thinking, perhaps muscle tension, as one can duplicate if they squeeze their eyes shut, was the cause of the flashes, I covered my eyes with my hands—thus allowing my eyes to be open. I was surprised that there was no feeling of difference with my eyes open and my hands cupped over my eyes, nor did the miles of darkness or the flashes alter.

"I could hear the participants of the study close to the

outside door—yet I was not aware of their presence. I was aware of a presence inside the pyramid, but distinctly not a person.

"I lapsed early into a feeling of great relaxation, and that ability as a general rule eludes me. Once I, sitting Yoga style on the chair, lifted my face to the center, my head tipped far back. I waited for the white star flashes that accompany pinching the nerve . . . but nothing happened and surprisingly when I tipped my head forward, chin on chest, nothing happened—no stars.

"Perhaps the strangest phenomenon for me was that not once during the experiment was I aware of time. Not 'how much longer,' 'how long have I been here,' 'how long have I sat with my legs crossed?' . . . nothing in terms of time. My first thought when I left the pyramid was 'Well, I'll be, I didn't once think of time.' It was something like a world-without-end feeling. It was with a half-smile that I realized that when the door had been opened, signaling that my time was up, I felt an intrusion, as if they were violating my space."

Thinking in terms of future research, there are a number of devices and instruments now being used in a variety of ways that may help us in understanding the energy fields within pyramids and energy fields in general.

Some supports for energy fields charted by divining techniques come from the development of energy-field detectors which show fields around the body as positively or negatively charged in different areas. Field polarities appear to change with hypnosis, meditation, anesthesia, sleep, and through the influence of external fields. The tobiscope and other biometers measure subtle changes in electrical resistance on the skin and are used to locate acupuncture points. Russian physicist Victor Adamenko has developed an instrument that picks up changes in body energy caused by alterations of consciousness and varying emotional states.

Force-field detectors developed in Russia by Dr. Genady Sergeyev have been classified as confidential by the military but have been reported as capable of detecting human energy fields up to a distance of four yards from the body. These may be similar to magnetic field detectors used in space research.

An American, David Thomson, has developed a human force-field detecting device that consists of two capacitor plates, a pre-amplifier, and a line recorder like that of an electrocardiograph. Thomson states that the detector charts the body's invisible electrical aura at some distance from the body. Working with Dr. Jack Ward, Thomson discovered that a person's force field detects the frequencies of the force fields of other people at a distance and is affected by them. Thomson stated, "People's force fields immediately sense fear, aggression, panic, or friendliness in another person." This work is under further study by Drs. Harold Kelm and Abram Hoffer at the University of Saskatchewan, Canada.

Research in force-field detectors is underway in Leningrad. Russia, at the Physiology Department. Dr. Pavel Gulyayev uses extremely sensitive high-resistance detection electrodes to chart the force field. Called the "electro-surogram," it reportedly is so sensitive it can measure the electrical field of a nerve. According to Gulyayev, the electrical emanations around the body change according to health, mood, character, and so on. He also reports that muscular reactions that accompany even a thought can be detected and that the signals in the electrical aura reveal a great deal about the state of the organism.

Forty years ago neuroanatomist Dr. Harold Saxton Burr of Yale University discovered that all living things, from plants to human, are controlled by electrodynamic fields. He measured these fields with standard modern voltmeters. Burr considered these fields of life—what he called "L-Fields"—to be the blueprints of life. Measuring L-Fields with voltmeters, he learned that illnesses such as cancer could be diagnosed before symptoms developed, and that the healing of both internal and external wounds could be monitored at a distance. He also found that internal processes such as ovulation could be accurately monitored according to changes in the electrodynamic fields of a woman's finger.

As with Kirlian researchers, Burr concluded that the energy matrix shapes the living form in matter. He discovered that there was a distinctive pattern of energies that would later form the blob of protoplasm into each element of the physical body. Rearranging the protoplasm apparently did not disrupt the final form.

Dr. Leonard Ravitz, a student of Burr, discovered that L-Fields also reflect people's mental states. As with Kirlian photography, the Burr approach revealed altered states of consciousness and changes in emotions. Ravitz learned that even the recollection of an emotion such as grief revealed an energy change of several millivolts as monitored by the voltmeter.

Burr believed that bodies and brains are maintained by permanent electromagnetic fields which mold the ever-changing material of the cells. These fields, in turn, are influenced by the greater fields of the universe and man is an integral part of the universe, sharing in its purpose and destiny. As a result of the development of new electronic instruments and techniques, "an entirely new approach to the nature of man and his place in the universe became possible," Burr stated.

The description of the human aura as provided by psychics and by means of Kirlian photography is very similar to observations by scientists studying heat-convection currents surrounding the human body. Normal body heat creates currents that form a vibrating envelope of warm air up to three inches thick. The layer is warmer than the general environment and shows up as a halo on photographic plates, using a nineteenth-century technique, called Schlieren photography, developed to detect flaws in glass. When convection currents are made visible by the Schlieren system, the envelope of warm air around the body appears as a pulsating, multicolored aura, Sheila Ostrander and Lynn Schroeder state in *Handbook of Psychic Discoveries*.

Researchers at City University of London, led by Dr.

Harold E. Lewis, found that the "heat" aura is laden with bacteria, particles of inorganic matter, and microscopic units of skin. According to these findings, the halos contain up to 400 percent more microorganisms than the immediate environment. Lewis theorized that some diseases may hang on because the envelope of warm air tends to trap bacteria and act as a breeding ground for them.

Schlieren photography reveals that convection currents in air can break up light into color patterns, and that each layer of air in the human air envelope has its own color. According to Lewis, the Schlieren technique reveals that, "Starting at the soles of the feet, the air layer moves slowly upward over the body. At the groin and under the armpits it reverses direction briefly. At the shoulders it spurts upward to dissipate in a feathery plume about five inches above the head." This description is strikingly similar to the psychic's perception of the halo.

The researchers discovered changes of color in the surrounding heat that coincided with an increased bacteria count due to infection and unusual changes in the flow pattern that coincided with areas of inflammation. Observing the flow pattern of the heat aura, the researchers found that the bacteria-laden warm air flowed toward the nose where it was inhaled. This led them to speculate that this process might account for certain bacterial and viral infections such as the asthma attacks children get after eczema. Arthritis, an illness in which the joints become inflamed, causes a rise in heat in certain areas and changes in the flow of convection currents. Doctors have now succeeded in mapping body temperatures with a heat-detecting instrument called a thermograph. This provides an early diagnosis approach for rheumatoid arthritis at the earliest, most crippling stage.

According to Dr. Glen W. McDonald of the U.S. Department of Health, Education and Welfare, the human body emits infrared radiation. "If the eyes were structured to see this emission," he stated, "each of us would have an incandescent glow." This glow can be seen by the thermograph. Areas of inflammation emit more heat than unaffected regions and their glow is different from normal glow.

The development of more sophisticated and sensitive instruments for the measurement of energy force fields and the recent interest in acupuncture has focused a growing amount of attention on the body's electrical system. If the body functions within an electrodynamic field, it is hypothesized that electromagnetic stimulation of the body could be beneficial if applied in the correct amount to raise the bioelectrical pulsation of the body's cells, tissue, and organs to their optimal level.

One of the pioneers in this field was George Lakhovsky, a Russian who did his research prior to World War II and died in this country in 1942. He invented the multiwave oscillator (MWO), a device that creates multiple electromagnetic waves that allegedly can be used to stimulate the body and repair damaged cells and tissues. While the MWO was used extensively in Europe at one time, it never caught hold in this country, partly due to the AMA's suspicion of radiobiological approaches. However, the new interest in bioelectric medicine may vindicate Lakhovsky.

Lakhovsky claimed that all cells capable of reproduction contain in their nuclei "filaments" of highly conductive material surrounded by insulating media. This filament, which may be the RNA-DNA complex, is always in the form of a spiral or helix, in other words, a coil. Therefore, each will react as a tuned circuit if its resonant frequency can be approximated by an external oscillating coil.

According to Bob Beck, who discussed his work with the device in the Borderland Sciences Research Foundation publication "The Lakhovsky MWO," Lakhovsky did not carry the matter to its conclusion. Beck postulated that "by exciting the nuclei with electromagnetic energy a 'charge' can be induced by the long established principle of electromagnetic induction. This demonstrably raises the energy level and perhaps the vitality of every cell in the field simultaneously. Since each cell is an individual, and of slightly different physical dimensions, the existing wavelengths must be multiple, and must span a broad frequency spectrum.

"The electromotive force (emf) produced by the MWO and induced in the cell nucleus, can raise the cell's metabolic rate by electrolysis, and perhaps jog the RNA-DNA 'memory' and reproductive capabilities to their level at an earlier, younger age, thus the rejuvenation . . ."

The multiwave oscillator radiates a bandwidth of radio-frequency energy from the audio frequencies up beyond microwave frequencies. By measurement with standard field-strength meters, this bandwidth of frequencies can be shown, and a bluish glow of brush discharge surrounds the antenna when operating. Within this multiple-wave range of frequencies, according to Beck, every cell in the body can find its one resonant frequency and absorb energy at its own natural wavelength.

An important piece of research documenting that pyramid energy increases plant growth was carried out during the fall of 1975 by Jack Dyer during the final semester of his senior year at Central State College in Edmund, Oklahoma. He became interested in pyramid phenomena and developed a plant-growth experiment for which he received credit in two of his classes, science and experimental psychology.

He chose sixty hybrid garden-type beans, as there would be very little difference in the seeds, and germinated them together in a tray. Two days later he selected the germinated seeds from a hopper without looking at them and placed them in identical containers. The seeds were planted in vermiculite compound and watered with carefully measured amounts. The containers were assigned to geometrical shapes by means of random assignment by a computer. The geometrical shapes consisted of pyramids, equilateral prisms, and rectangles. Five boxes of each shape were constructed from single-strength glass and each box had a volume of 361.1 cubic inches. Three seed containers were assigned to each of the glass boxes. Fifteen additional seed containers were used as controls and not placed inside glass boxes. They were placed on the same shelves, however, and provided identical growing conditions. All plants were exposed to fluorescent Gro-lite lighting for sixteen hours each day. In addition to the experimental and control seeds, three of the germinated seeds were placed in each of three geometrical shapes, along with a fourth seed used as a control, and these were placed on separate window sills. The glass boxes were held together by aquarium glue but none were sealed all the way to the apex so that air could circulate. All were glued an equal distance on the sides. The experiment took place in a pre-stress concrete building on the top floor of a two-story building.

The plants were grown from November 29 until December 9. Their growth rate to one-thousandths of an inch was then measured by means of a micrometer. The height of the plant and the diameter of the stalk were measured, and those two measurements were added together. The following figures show the growth rate in inches of each plant in each group, the mean or average growth rate, and the total growth for all plants in each group:

Plants	Control	Rectangle	Prism	Pyramid
# 1	4.138	3.746	5.677	5.732
# 2	3.539	4.041	4.528	7.435
# 3	2.223	4.241	3.829	5.668
# 4	5.055	5.826	6.444	7.358
# 5	5.854	5.546	5.541	6.538
# 6	1.151	2.764	6.950	7.252
# 7	6.531	6.350	7.842	6.653
# 8	6.032	5.139	3.550	4.447
# 9	5.301	0.740	4.253	6.360
# 10	5.735	6.635	4.341	6.144
# 11	5.143	6.245	5.735	5.150
# 12	2.628	4.126	1.529	5.654
# 13	4.932	5.146	7.308	6.150
# 14	4.143	1.324	3.739	4.622
# 15	0.001	3.294	3.150	4.470
Total Growth	62.406	65.163	74.416	89.633
Average Growth Rate	4.1604	4.3442	4.96107	5.97553

As can be seen, the pyramid plants handily outgrew the others; the prism was next; the rectangle third, and the control plants last.

"This was quite a difference in the growth rates," Dyer told us. "This is statistically significant. I'm impressed and I was really skeptical when I first went into this. This certainly warrants further investigation and I plan to do more, as well as further data analysis on this one."

Dyer explained that the computer was used to make daily location selections for the plants in order that each plant received equal treatment as regards light, heat, air circulation, and so on.

When the experiment was completed, the computer indicated there was "significant growth rate difference," rather than this being a conclusion reached by himself.

The windowsill samples, incidentally, were much

slower in growing, which is understandable as they were exposed only to sunlight, which is of short duration during November and December. However, the pyramid plants again outgrew the others and again the prism was second; the rectangle third, and the control last.

Dyer discovered a rather curious thing when he weighed the plants. When the plants were pulled and the wet weight (green) measured on a gram scale, the pyramid plants were the heaviest. Yet, after being dried in an herbal dryer, the pyramid plants weighed the least and the control plants, which weighed the least as wet weight, weighed the most as dry weight!

We are constantly being amazed at the variety of phenomena produced by pyramids. One wonders in what fields of endeavor the pyramid does not apply. Joe Wall of Milwaukee, Wisconsin, recently wrote to us of his discovery of the use of pyramids in the treatment of paints, solvents, and so forth. The implications for industry appear promising.

"I work with electrostatic paint-spraying equipment," Wall states. "The solvent that is added to thin the paints must be in the 'Keystone' class, that is, the Acetones, Methyl Ethyl Keystones, MIBK, Isophorenes, etc., are 'polar' solvents to attract the paint particles to apply more paint to the object. These solvents must carry a 20 microamp charge at the tip of the gun to electrify these paint particles. All the Keystones treated in the pyramid for four weeks now carry a microamp charge of 50 microamps. In other words, the solvents are highly polar after treatment in the pyramids.

"Now, here's one that astounds me. The aromatic solvents are what I call 'dead' solvents—not polar. These solvents are very cheap but can't be added to electrostatic equipment because they do not generate a charge. After four weeks in the pyramid, these solvents—Teleul, Xylol, Milsolves, etc.—now carry a 20 microamp charge and can be used for electrostatic spraying. This is great because the Keystones are three times the cost of the 'hydro-carbons' or aromatic solvents and certainly will reduce paint costs to the consumer."

I was preparing to write a conclusion to this chapter when a friend, a physician, called. "Something has just happened here that I think you would be interested in," he said.

He explained that a friend, a director of a mental-health clinic, had dropped by his office, was not feeling well, and they had decided to do some work on him with auricular therapy. The physician shot Kirlian photos before and after the treatment. The results of the treatment were definitely reflected in the pictures. "But we had a thought about trying the pyramids in some fashion," he explained, but as a large enough pyramid for the patient to sit in was not available, they decided to have him hold two small metal plates that had been charged in a pyramid. He held the plates, one in each hand, for five minutes, and then Kirlian photos were again taken of his fingertips. The photos reveal a considerable difference. The coronas were much brighter and there were fewer breaks in the pattern.

Interesting results with fish in an aquarium were produced by Tom Garrett of Oklahoma City. He placed a six-inch cardboard pyramid underneath the tank and within ten days the fish started dying. Garrett lost seven, including several of his expensive guppies, before he removed the pyramid. No more of the fish died, although a brown stain, which had formed on the sides of the tank and on the polished gravel in the bottom, remained. The water had turned murky.

Garrett then placed a three-inch cast plastic pyramid inside the tank on top of the gravel. Within hours the water started clearing and within a few days the stain started clearing from the sides of the tank and the gravel. The fish became very active, turned a brighter color, particularly the fanzitail guppies. They reproduced very rapidly, and whereas usually only two guppies will survive out of a hatch, Garrett estimated that six or more are surviving. The fish have also become very tame and can be hand fed. After the water cleared, Garrett removed the Dynaflo filtering system from the tank and yet a month later, at this writing, the water has remained clear and the fish healthy.

One interesting speculation—and it is certainly nothing more than this—concerns the fish dying when the pyramid was placed beneath the aquarium. It was recently reported by divers that a large stone pyramid exists beneath the surface of the water somewhere within the Bermuda Triangle where so many ships and planes have allegedly disappeared. Could it be that if the sides of the pyramid are extended they form an invisible inverted pyramid directly above, apex to apex, and this is an anti-pyramid producing a destructive instead of a constructive force?

Pyramid research is important. Results of experiments to date are exciting and promising. It has been amply demonstrated that the geometrical space in which an activity is enclosed will modify the result. We have learned a little about the shape of this space and we know something about how to produce a desired result. A great deal more remains to be learned, of course, and quite likely we have only scratched the surface. But we have a few guidelines, some directions, a bit of data, and some combinations that will open additional doors. It is a beginning.

The words of Dr. William Tiller apply. When speaking on "Energy Fields and the Human Body" at the Symposium on Mind-Body Relationships in the Disease Process held in Phoenix in January 1972, he urged his audience to support the scientific exploration of the newly discovered dimensions of the human being and his environment. Pyramid research qualifies.

He stated, ". . . I think we can really start now. We now have a few tools, not many as yet nor are they well understood; however, there are some that will let us transform this information to a level of understanding that is meaningful to our society. As we start such experiments, we will begin to see deeper and deeper into these aspects of Nature, and all the hidden treasures that are never anticipated in the initial model are in store for us just below the surface of our present understanding."

## 15

The Esoteric Pyramid

"It is the pupils of those incarnated Rishis and Devas of the Third Root Race, who handed their knowledge from one generation to another, to Egypt and Greece with its now lost canon of proportion; as it is the Disciples of the Initiates of the 4th, the Atlanteans, who handed it over to their Cyclops, the 'Sons of Cycles' or of the 'Infinite,' from whom the name passed to the still later generations of Gnostic priests. It is owing to the divine perfection of those architectural proportions that the Ancients could build those wonders of all the subsequent ages, their Fanes, Pyramids, Cave-Temples, Cromlechs, Cairns, Altars, proving they had the powers of machinery and a knowledge of mechanics to which modern skill is like a child's play, and which that skill refers to itself as the 'works of hundred-handed giants,'" H. P. Blavatsky states in the abridgment of *The Secret Doctrine.*

She continues in the footnote to Stanza 6:

"Modern architects may not altogether have neglected those rules, but they have superadded enough empirical innovations to destroy those just proportions. It is Vitruvius who gave to posterity the rules of construction of the Grecian temples erected to the immortal Gods; and the ten books of Marcus Vitruvius Pollio on Architecture, of one, in short, who was an initiate, can only be studied esoterically. The Druidical circles, the Dolmens, the Temples of India, Egypt and Greece, the Towers and the 127 towns in Europe which were found 'Cyclopean in origin' by the French Institute, are all the work of initiated Priest-architects, the descendants of those primarily taught by the 'Sons of Gods,' justly called 'the Builders.' This is what appreciative posterity says of those descendants. 'They used neither mortar nor cement, nor steel nor iron to cut the stones with; and yet they were so artfully wrought that in many places the joints are not seen, though many of the stones, as in Peru, are 18 feet thick, and in the walls of the fortress of Cuzco there are stones of a still greater size.' "

Occult literature abounds with intriguing tales of the great pyramids of Gizeh, their origin, their designers, the reasons for their construction. This body of literature is too voluminous, even in regard to the nature and purpose of the Great Pyramid, to consider here even in outline form. It is mentioned, however, for several reasons and the above was quoted from *The Secret Doctrine* to indicate the nature of this literature to those who are not familiar with it.

A number of people have asked us and we have received many letters inquiring as to why we have not made greater reference to this material in our writings on pyramids. The reason such inquiries are made is that occult literature offers answers to the many questions surrounding the pyramids, the Sphinx, Stonehenge, and so on, and those familiar with this tradition suggest greater reference to it.

Unfortunately, the word "occult" has been unfairly attacked recently by some critics. It is a perfectly good word, meaning both "hidden" and "esoteric," depending on how it is used. However, there have been some grave abuses committed in the name of the occult . . . misleading, even damaging information given to people through the press, classes, workshops, and so forth. Many people have of late become interested in learning about expanded states of awareness, paranormal powers, and exploring extra dimensions of the human being. All legitimate pursuits, but in their enthusiasm to reach for the greater realization of the self they have innocently become involved with some of the less desirable elements of this movement and have been misled for lack of developed powers of discrimination.

The "occult" has shouldered much of the blame and some legitimate factions of the occult have been unjustly censored by those who also cannot discriminate. By way of illustration, there are ways of unusual breathing that can be beneficial to the physical body, can have a calming effect on the emotions and mind, and can be of real assistance to the person learning control over internal states of awareness. However, when such exercises are improperly taught and therefore improperly practiced they can be distressing and even dangerous to the practitioner. Sadly enough, there are persons with inadequate training themselves who continue to compound this error by teaching others.

There are also many excellent schools and centers teaching students philosophical concepts, practical, moral, and ethical application of principles, and providing a discipline of growth that can be of benefit to themselves and others. A number of these schools make regular use of a body of literature that they may refer to as the occult.

But all things are not equal within the occult, as there is valued and worthless literature in most fields. Some of the occult material has been handed down for centuries, constantly being tested along the way as to its benefit to mankind, and much of it is now being confirmed by the scientific method. Other occult literature falls basically into two categories: material that bears some accuracy in the sense that it works but is such that it develops skills or strengths that have to do with the lower nature of man and works toward greed, lust, selfishness, perverted power, and the manipulation of others. One of the more graphic examples of the black magician in recent history was Adolf Hitler, a man of great intellect and magnetism who used this power against the world. The second branch of occult literature to be avoided is that mumbo-jumbo uttered by persons who have discovered it to be an easy ripoff, who are laboring under grandiose delusions, or who innocently but ignorantly write, speak, or teach from material they believe of value.

Legitimate occult knowledge has a respected heritage. Based upon the he-who-has-ears-let-him-hear tradition, it considers that some persons are more advanced in their understanding than others. For the most part, occult literature is derived from individuals or groups who received information through mystical or intuitive channels. Having experienced a temporary or sustained level of elevated consciousness, they allegedly were the recipients of information not available to the average person. This knowledge was then passed on to others who were believed ready to receive it. Endeavoring to protect this body of knowledge from the ignorant who might abuse it, as well as from those who might feel threatened and therefore attempt to destroy it, the teachers established schools for a selected few aspirants. These schools became known in time as the "Mystery Schools." They accepted students whom they considered qualified and allegedly taught these initiates how to develop higher powers of perception and functioning.

Some fragments of Mystery Schools are still in existence but those knowing of these sites are not free to reveal their location or their teachings. There are other schools, organizations, and centers whose teachings are based upon this knowledge. There have been down through the ages highly advanced teachers who have instructed a small group of selected followers in one fashion and the public in a manner acceptable to their level of understanding. There is a legend surrounding the origin of the Mystery Schools and the sinking of the continent of Atlantis. According to this story, the inhabitants of that fabled land had reached a highly sophisticated level of paranormal development and a control over energy fields and their environment. There were those, however, who endeavored to use their talents to grab power. The ensuing struggle between the "black magicians" and the "white magicians" resulted in the eventual destruction of their land. The survivors, who had migrated to other lands, swore that never again would this knowledge be imparted to the public at large; aspirants would have to demonstrate abilities to correctly make use of the teachings before they were made accessible. The candidates would be given only such information as they were prepared to use wisely. As others might demand this knowledge and even use force to obtain it, the schools became secret and the Mystery Schools were born.

Of these Mystery Schools, Manly Palmer Hall states in *The Secret Teachings of All Ages* (an encyclopedic outline of Masonic, Hermetic, Qabbalistic and Rosicrucian symbolical philosophy):

"From indisputable facts such as these it is evident that philosophy emerged from the religious Mysteries of Antiquity not being separated from religion until after the decay of the Mysteries. Hence he who would fathom the depths of philosophic thought must familiarize himself with the teachings of those initiated priests designated to be the guardians of a transcendental knowledge so profound as to be incomprehensible save to the most exalted intellect and so potent as to be revealed with safety only to those in whom personal ambition was dead and who had consecrated their lives to the unselfish service of humanity. Both the dignity of these sacred institutions and the validity of their claim to possession of Universal Wisdom are attested by the most illustrious philosophers of antiquity, who were themselves initiated into the profundities of the secret doctrine and who bore witness to its efficacy."

Later in the Introduction, Hall states, "Far-sighted were the initiates of antiquity. They realized that nations come and go, that empires rise and fall, and that the golden ages of art, science, and idealism are succeeded by the dark ages of superstition. With the needs of posterity foremost in mind, the sages of old went to inconceivable extremes to make certain that their knowledge should be preserved. They engraved it upon the face of mountains and concealed it within the measurements of colossal images, each of which was a geometric marvel. Their knowledge of chemistry and mathematics they hid within mythologies which the ignorant would perpetuate, or in the spans and arches of their temples which time has not entirely obliterated. They wrote in characters that neither the vandalism of men nor the ruthlessness of the elements could completely efface. Today men gaze with awe and reverence upon the mighty Memnons standing alone on the sands of Egypt, or upon the strange terraced pyramids of Palanque. Mute testimonies these are of the lost arts and sciences of antiquity; and concealed this wisdom must remain until this race has learned to read the universal language—Symbolism."

Hall provides in the chapter "The Initiation of the Pyramid" the tradition of the Mysteries as to the purpose of the Great Pyramid, the symbolism in its design, and the nature of the initiations that took place within its chambers. It is much too long to quote here and to select passages would too severely alter the picture as presented. But it is recommended reading, although the chapter should be read along with the rest of the book to do it justice.

The question likely to be raised at this time is, "Do we, then, accept this body of knowledge regarding the Great Pyramid as accurate?"

There can be no unequivocal answer offered for a variety of reasons. An attendent question to the above would be, "To what extent did the Mysteries ascertain Truth?" Our first problem in providing an answer is determining whether the Mysteries were accurate as originally given, and if this question can be answered in the affirmative, then me must muse on what has been lost through time, intellectual erosion, translation, and so forth. Then, in regard to the above reference, to what degree was Hall capable of researching and pulling together this body of knowledge? Questions to which there are no easy answers, for the moment that we launch our research the same questions have to be applied to us including our level of comprehension, which in this case must also incorporate mystical talents. So the problems become compounded. At any time that we feel the psychological need to gain closure, we can make some choices in answers but we should be willing in such a case to admit that we have arrived at them arbitrarily.

Is there no way, then, to close the gate? Probably not. But human nature being what it is we will keep on trying. And there are ways to try. However, we should not perhaps place too much hope on hidden documents in subterranean chambers. Even if found and decodable, we would have to raise the same set of questions: Who placed the documents there? Did they know? How do we know they have been translated accurately? The same unavoidable games, played over again with every discovered artifact, every piece of so-called sacred literature, and as recently experienced with the Dead Sea Scrolls.

There are contemporary psychics who tell us they have received information as to the construction and purpose of the Great Pyramid. Do we accept this information? Again, it is a matter of choice. It helps if all psychics are in agreement and if their collective information coincides with that of past mystics. Unfortunately, this isn't entirely the case. What we can do, however, is find those areas of closest agreement and work from there in an eclectic fashion to pull the puzzle together as best we can. This knowledge can be weighed against the latest scientific evidence and herein research with pyramid models can make a real contribution.

In the end we stand alone with our questions, each of us the guardian of his own truths. The pyramid once again has referred us back to ourselves, telling us that the knowledge rests within. When we understand ourselves well enough—having elevated our awareness to consciousness itself perhaps—we will understand the pyramid, realizing that what was hidden all along was the observer.

APPENDIX I

Construction of Pyramid Models

Since the publication of *The Secret Power of Pyramids* we have received many inquiries about the construction of pyramid models. Some have explained that the instructions we gave were confusing to them, as they were not used to working with degrees and decimals.

One way to determine the measurements is to multiply the desired height of the pyramid by 1.57 to obtain the figure for the base, and multiply the height by 1.49 to obtain the figure for the sides. When the four identical triangles are leaned together, they form the correct pyramid. By this method one does not have to be concerned with figuring angles.

In order to simplify further, one can use the following measurements and double, triple, and so on to get the desired size:

Height	Base	Sides
6″	9⅜″	8⅞″
8″	12⅝″	12″
10″	15¾″	15″
12″	18¾″	17¾″
8′	12′ 6″	12′
6′	9′ 5″	8′ 11″

Some people, however, would rather not use measurements at all, so we are including a pattern that is sufficiently accurate for most purposes. The following pattern is for the apex of the pyramid; use it as a pattern and simply extend the sides equally to the desired length, whether this is two inches or ten feet. Connect the two sides with a new base line and you have the pyramid triangle. Make four of these triangles; fasten them together and your pyramid is ready for experiments.

Many people have expressed an interest in pyramids of various sizes, their main concern being "Is the pyramid force stronger inside a large pyramid than a small one?"

Of course, size is relative depending on what is to be placed inside the pyramid. So many variables are involved that it is difficult to differentiate between various sizes. Undoubtedly, this is an area where more research is required and the best suggestion that we can offer at this time is that the pyramid should be large enough so that the mass of the object or subject is located in the center of the pyramid. We have found, from interviews with many people, that headaches seem to be reduced or eliminated, and other healing processes noted, regardless of the size of the pyramid, but that method is too intangible to be usable as a guide.

We decided to try to determine what difference in effect various sizes and composition of pyramids would have on homogenized milk, as it is one of the most unpredictable items that we have used in our experiments. The following tests were run between July and November 1975. The figures are averages from numerous tests, each of six days duration:

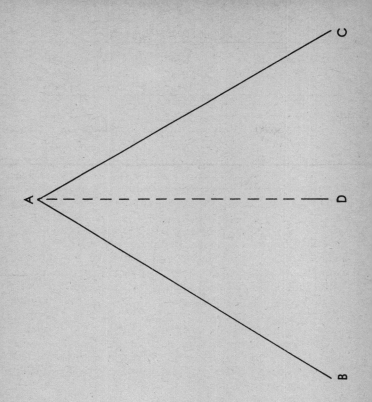

Extend lines A-B and A-C to equal lengths as per opposite page. Connect extended lines to form base of triangle.

Example: If desired pyramid height is to be 6", multiply 6" x 1.49 = 8.9" (sides A-B and A-C).

Note: Line A-D will not equal height of completed pyramid.

Pyramid Size	Material	Location in Pyramid	Results
10"	Glass	King's Chamber	Smooth yogurt, no mold
12"	Silvered mirror	King's Chamber	Stratified, sour
16"	Wood sides, glass front	King's Chamber	Smooth yogurt, no mold
72"	Wood frame—polyethylene cover	2 inches above apex	No mold, no stratification
72"	Same as above	2 inches below apex	Same as above
72"	Same as above	King's Chamber	Smooth yogurt, no mold
10½'	Wood fiber, glass insulation	4 inches below apex	About one-half yogurt consistency, no mold
10½'	Same as above	King's Chamber	Smooth yogurt, no mold

Milk placed on open shelf without pyramid

In jar only .... stratification, moldy

In jar covered with foil treated in pyramid .... no change, sweet smell, no stratification, no mold

Normally, milk will turn to yogurt inside pyramids in from four to six days; however, the time will vary for unknown reasons even though temperature and humidity are controlled. At times milk will only stratify and sometimes sour under seemingly identical conditions. The above tests consisted of placing three ounces of milk from the same container into four-ounce glass jars that were sterilized. There are times when milk will turn to yogurt within 24 to 48 hours while on other occasions, for reasons unknown—sunspot activity, geomagnetism, or whatever —milk will turn to yogurt in one pyramid, while in another pyramid of the same size and composition the milk will sour. More than likely this could not be accounted for through sunspot activity, but we might speculate that there is a correlation between sunspot activity and the earth's magnetism which is known to fluctuate considerably in various spots in a comparatively short period of time. We have had such differences occur when the pyramids were as close together as one hundred feet and as far away as nine miles.

From the various tests that we have run with milk, we would suggest that the most ideal material for the composition of the pyramid would be wood (smooth); the second best is cardboard; third, plastic (not porous); fourth, silvered mirror, which is not recommended; and, fifth, metal, which also is not recommended.

While our experiments indicate that slight errors in measurement do not appreciably alter the results, some researchers are sticklers for accuracy and are bothered if ten-thousandths of an inch is ignored. We can honor them for their insistence on mathematical perfection but we find it difficult to live up to their expectations with tape measure and skillsaw.

But for those who fancy seeing figures stretching into infinity on the right side of the decimal point, the following letter from a faculty member of a well-known university will award them with a certain degree of ecstasy:

"I have just purchased a copy of 'The Secret Power of Pyramids' and, as yet, have only read that small section having to do with constructing small pyramids. I wish to point out a trap which you fell into.

"Accuracy is the name-of-the-game with the Great Pyramid—it was constructed to an accuracy to or greater than our ability to measure it. One of the most difficult measures to determine is its height. This difficulty arises because of the missing capstone and missing casing stones, therefore, the height dimension must be extrapolated.

"The dimensions you give on page 197 are very good dimensions; however, they are for a pyramid designed by use of Pi in which the height is obtained by dividing the perimeter by 2 Pi. This design philosophy has been adopted by several prominent pyramidologists and promulgated by several authors of literature on the pyramids. The erroneous belief resulted from two factors: (1) rounding numbers to four places, and (2) assuming that the ancient builders came close to knowing the value of Pi as we know it.

"I have just completed a rigorous analysis of the Great Pyramid of Gizeh to 10-place accuracy and can argue successfully that the pyramid was built in accordance with the ancient golden geometrical section, Phi. A result of this analysis is disclosure of how easily one can fall into a trap in playing the numbers game.

"For example, if the Great Pyramid had been designed by the function Pi, one would have a height of 1.273 239 545 relative units. If one designed by the golden section, Phi, one gets 1.272 019 650 relative units.

"The difference is small, like 0.0959%, but it can be shown that the actual pyramid was dimensioned to an accuracy of 8 parts in 1 million parts, or to within 0.0008%.

"Your dimensions, therefore, are 0.0959% too long for the height and the sides. If you really want to be accurate, take the base (any length desired in any units of measure) as the reference. Then do the following:

"Base times 0.636 009 825 equals height.

"Base times 0.809 016 994 5 equals length of one face from the center of its base to its apex.

"Base times 0.951 056 5165 equals length of one edge from one corner to the apex.

"Your corrected table, using the base length as given in your book, should read:

Height	Base	Side
2.9956"	4.71"	4.4795"
3.9941	6.28	5.9726
4.9927	7.85	7.3992
7.8992	12.42	11.8121
9.9854	15.70	14.9316
11.9888	18.85	17.9274

Whether or not we are attracted to the mathematical equations of the pyramid, one can't help but be awed at the fantastic accuracy of the ancient builders. If they were capable of that caliber of mathematics, architecture, engineering, and construction, what else did they know? This question can't help but haunt our thoughts as we set up our experiments with pyramid models.

APPENDIX II

Razor Blade Experiments

A worthwhile research design for measuring the effectiveness of pyramids to keep razor blades sharp has been devised by Major Charles W. Dutreau of Stillwater, Oklahoma.

Dutreau, a retired Army research chemist, is now involved in the design of underground buildings of various types and residencies. He became interested in pyramid research after obtaining more shaves from razor blades placed in pyramids. He invited other scientists, engineers, and educators to participate in the project and recruited twenty-five for the initial experiment. He constructed twenty-five cardboard pyramids approximately 10 centimeters in height and gave them to subjects, along with instructions for their use. Each of the pyramids had fixed pedestals on which to place the razor blades.

The project was divided into the "Control phase" and "Determinant phase." In the instructions to the subjects Major Dutreau asked them to keep all variables the

SURVIVAL ENGINEERS OF OKLAHOMA

P. O. Box 1256

ID No. ——— Stillwater, Oklahoma 74074

SEO Experiment No. 76–001

PURPOSE: To determine whether the shaving performance of safety razor blades significantly is influenced by storage between uses in a cardboard pyramid under controlled conditions.

Record of Performance

Performance Code: Excellent-1, Good-2, Fair-3, Poor-4, Non-usable-5

Shave No.	Date	Code No.	Shave No.	Date	Code No.	Shave No.	Date	Code No.	Shave No.	Date	Code No.
1			18			35			52		
2			19			36			53		
3			20			37			54		
4			21			38			55		
5			22			39			56		
6			23			40			57		
7			24			41			58		
8			25			42			59		
9			26			43			60		
10			27			44			61		
11			28			45			62		
12			29			46			63		
13			30			47			64		
14			31			48			65		
15			32			49			66		
16			33			50			67		
17			34			51			68		

same—that is, tension on the blade in an adjustable razor, the same lather, and so on. After shaving with the control blade the subjects were asked to remove the blade from the razor, blow off the excess water, and place it in a dry spot away from light. The experimental blade was to be treated in an identical manner but returned to the pyramid after shaving.

The subjects were asked to keep a log on their shaving experiences by marking data sheets on which were recorded the performance on a scale of 1 to 5: 1-Excellent, 2-Good, 3-Fair, 4-Poor, and 5-Non-usable. Once the blades were non-usable, they were to be wrapped in tissue paper and mailed to Major Dutreau.

As this project was scheduled to get underway as we were preparing to go to press with this book, the results were not known. It is included here, however, to indicate the growing interest in pyramid research and to illustrate the manner in which experiments can be initiated.

SURVIVAL ENGINEERS OF OKLAHOMA
P. O. Box 1256
Stillwater, Oklahoma 74074
18 Jan 76

Instructions to Participants in SEO Experiment No. 76–001
(Code Name—Operation Razor Blade)

This operation will be executed in two phases—1) the Control Phase and 2) the Determinant Phase. The same safety razor will be used and the same shaving practices adhered to throughout the experiment.

Control Phase

1. Remove one of the enclosed double-edged blades from the wrapper and affix it in the head of your razor. Adjustable razor heads should be set at the desired tension and not changed for the duration of the experiment. Be sure that the handle is tightened all the way while shaving.

2. Wash and lather the face and shave in the normal way,

using the same soap or shaving preparation throughout the experiment. Do not use the blade for trimming your beard or mustache. Remove the blade from the razor after each use. Blow off the excess water (do not wipe) and keep it in a dry place away from light.

3. Using Data Sheet No. 1, record the date and performance code of the blade after each shave. Rate the performance on a scale of 1 to 5:—1-Excellent, 2-Good, 3-Fair, 4-Poor, and 5-Non-Usable. Be as objective as possible in the evaluation of each performance.

4. When the blade becomes "non-usable," wrap it in a piece of tissue and mail it to Survival Engineers of Oklahoma, along with the completed data sheet. Use the enclosed stamped and pre-addressed envelope marked "Data Sheet No. 1." Then begin the "Determinant Phase."

Determinant Phase

1. Place the pyramid base furnished herewith on a level surface where it will not be disturbed, and where it will not be near any electrical appliance. The arrow in the base should point directly north.

2. Remove the second blade from the wrapper and insert it in the same razor used in the control phase. Wash and lather the face and shave in the normal way, observing the same shaving practices as with the first blade.

3. Remove the blade from the razor after each use, blow off the excess water (do not wipe) and place it on the platform located in the center of the base. The ends will point north and south while the cutting edges face east and west. Cover the blade with the pyramid, fitting it into the guides secured to the base. Leave the blade in place until the next use and repeat the above routine.

4. Record the date and performance code of the blade after each use, using Data Sheet No. 2.

5. When the blade becomes "non-usable," wrap it in tissue and mail it, along with the data sheet, to Survival Engineers. Use the remaining envelope marked "Data Sheet No. 2."

Explanatory Notes

Independent experiments have reported that razor blades stored between uses at a certain point within a pyramidal structure seem to retain their sharpness through a significantly greater number of uses than blades stored in the usual places, such as a drawer or the shelf of a medicine cabinet. Small pyramids of cardboard or plastic are being sold for this purpose in several European countries.

This and other reports of mysterious "Pyramid Power" are so fantastic and illogical that few scientists will bother to investigate them. However, the razor blade phenomenon has been reported so frequently and persistently from so many sources that we believe the time has come for a determination, once and for all, whether the claims are fraudulent or valid.

Names of participants in this experiment, as well as raw data supplied by individuals, will be kept confidential by the research agency. Data sheets are identified by number only. However, participants are free to discuss their observations freely if they desire to do so.

Upon completion of the experiment, data will be subjected to statistical analysis and a report furnished to all participants. If the studies should indicate a significant difference in razor blade performance during the control phase and the determinant phase, then—in that event—consideration will be given to a research project designed to explore in depth the findings derived therefrom.

Please be completely honest, objective and non-emotional in recording your observations.

Thank you for finding time in your busy life to join in our search for the elusive Truth.

Sincerely,

CHARLES W. DUTREAU
Director

Water Experiment

Measuring differences in trace minerals in treated and untreated water has been another one of those experiences that are baffling. Again, it has left us with more questions than answers. The findings are significant. How significant future research must determine.

Close to the midnight hour of completing this book we ran trace mineral tests on Pettit's tap water. In one test, the water was treated for 13 hours and compared to the control water drawn at the same time and kept in an identical sterilized tube. In the second test, water was used that had been kept in a pyramid for two weeks, and it was compared to control water drawn at the same time. The tests were run in the laboratory of the Center For Improving Human Functioning in Wichita, Kansas. The following table shows the decrease in the amounts of copper and zinc in the treated water. The water used in the 13-hour test did not show any copper in either sample.

	Copper parts per million	Zinc parts per million
13-Hour Test		
Treated Water	0	.54
Untreated Water	0	.80
Two-Week Test		
Treated Water	.01	.01
Untreated Water	.09	.13

We plan to run a number of trace mineral tests and in future experiments the water will be standardized by adding a determined amount of copper, iron, and zinc to the water. It will then be divided into control and experimental samples.

Bibliography

Beck, B. "The Lakhovsky MWO," Borderland Sciences Research Foundation Publication. Vista, California.

Blavatsky, H. P. *The Secret Doctrine*. Los Angeles: Theosophical Society, 1930.

Brena, S. *Yoga and Medicine*. New York: Julian Press, 1972.

Brunton, P. *The Secret Path*. New York: E. P. Dutton and Co., 1935.

Brunton, P. *The Wisdom of the Overself*. New York: E. P. Dutton and Co., 1943.

Bucke, R. M. *Cosmic Consciousness*. New York: E. P. Dutton and Co., 1964.

Burr, H. *The Fields of Life*. New York: Ballantine, 1973.

Carrington, H. *Yoga Philosophy*. Girard, Kans.: Haldemann-Julius, 1923.

Castaneda, C. *The Teachings of Don Juan*. Berkeley: University of California Press, 1968.

Chardin, T. *The Phenomenon of Man*. New York: Harper and Row.

Eiseley, L. *The Invisible Pyramid*. New York: Charles Scribner's Sons, 1970.

Evans-Wentz, W. Y. *The Fairy Faith in Celtic Countries*. London: Henry Frowde, 1911.

Frei, E. H. "Medical Applications of Magnetism," *Bulletin of the Atomic Scientists,* October 1972.

Gauquelin, M. *Cosmic Clocks*. London: Peter Owen, 1969.

Hall, M. P. *The Secret Teachings of All Ages*. Los Angeles: Philosophical Research Society, 1969.

Hauschka, R. *The Nature of Substance*. London: Stuart & Watkins, 1966.

Heindel, M. *Cosmo-Conception*. Oceanside, Calif.: Rosicrucian Fellowship, 1911.

Huxley, A. *Brave New World.*

Huxley, A. *Doors of Perception*. New York: Harper and Row, 1954.

James, W. *Varieties of Religious Experience*. London: Longmans, Green & Co., 1902.

Karlins, M. and Andrews, L. M. *Biofeedback*. New York: Warner, 1972.

Kerrell, B., and Goggin, K. *The Guide to Pyramid Energy*. Santa Monica, Calif., 1975.

Kervran, L. *Biological Transmutations*. Binghamton, N. Y.: Swan House, 1972.

Kohn, H. E. *Reflections*. Grand Rapids, Mich.: William B. Eerdmans, 1963.

Krishna, G. *Awakening of the Kundalini*. New York: E. P. Dutton and Co., 1975.

Krishna, G. *Higher Consciousness*. New York: Julian Press, 1974.

Michell, J. *View Over Atlantis*. New York: Ballantine Books, 1969.

Monroe, R. A. *Journeys Out of the Body*. New York: Doubleday, 1973.

Ostrander, S., and Schroeder, L. *Handbook of Psychic Discoveries*. New York: Berkeley, 1974.

Ostrander, S., and Schroeder, L. *Psychic Discoveries Behind the Iron Curtain*. Englewood Cliffs, N. J.: Prentice-Hall, 1970.

Piccardi, G. *The Chemical Basis of Medical Climatology*. Springfield, Ill.: Charles C. Thomas, 1962.

Pierrakos, J. C., "The Energy Field in Man and Nature," New York: Institute of Bioenergetic Analysis.

Powell, A. E. *The Etheric Double*. Wheaton, Ill.: Theosophical Publishing House, 1925.

Ramacharaka. *The Practical Water Cure*. Chicago: The Yogi Publishing Society, 1909.

Sadoul, J. *Alchemists and Gold*. New York: G. P. Putnam's Sons, 1972.

Schul, B., and Pettit, E. *The Secret Power of Pyramids*. Greenwich, Conn.: Fawcett Publications, 1975.

Skinner, B. F. *Beyond Freedom and Dignity*. New York: Knopf, 1971.

Tiller, W. A. "Radionics, Radiesthesia and Physics," unpublished paper.

Toben, B. *Space, Time and Beyond*. New York: E. P. Dutton and Co., 1975.

Tompkins, P. *Secrets of the Great Pyramid*. New York: Harper and Row, 1971.

Tompkins, P., and Bird, C. *The Secret Life of Plants*. New York: Avon, 1973.

Toth, M., and Nielsen, G. *Pyramid Power*. New York: Freeway Press, 1974.

Ullman, M., Krippner, S., and Vaughan, A. *Dream Telepathy*. New York: Macmillan, 1973.

Vishnudevananda. *The Complete Book of Yoga*. New York: Julian Press, New York, 1960.

Vivekananda. *Raja Yoga*. New York: Ramakrishna-Vivekananda Center, 1955.

Watson, L. *Super Nature*. New York: Doubleday, 1973.

Index